# Astronomy/Cosmology Breakthroughs and the God Question

## Proceedings of the ITEST Symposium September, 2007

ITEST
Institute for Theological Encounter with Science and Technology
Cardinal Rigali Center
20 Archbishop May Drive
Suite 3400A
St. Louis, Missouri 63119
USA

Published by:

ITEST Faith/Science Press
Institute for Theological Encounter with Science and Technology
Cardinal Rigali Center
20 Archbishop May Drive
Suite 3400A
St. Louis, Missouri 63119
USA

Phone: 314.792.7220
Email: ITEST-Info @ faithscience.org
Web Site: www.faithscience.org

Printed in the United States

ISBN: 1-885583 - 15-X

*Book typesetting and layout: Graphic Masters - Bill Herberholt*

*The cover is an original design by Mr. Leonard F. Buckley of Hanover, Pennsylvania. The artist has attempted to combine the theme into an image of a stained glass window. The three circular segments of the window, as well as the triangular center portion allude to the Trinity, the "Creator of Heaven and Earth, of all that is seen and unseen." The rendering of the spiral galaxy alludes to the discoveries of worlds in deep space. It is based upon the Whirlpool Galaxy NGC 5194, 37 million light years from our view here on Earth.*

*Mr. Buckley, retired foreman of Designers at the Bureau of Engraving and Printing, designed among other stamps the issue commemorating the Apollo 8 Flight as well as the mineral issues and California Statehood. He also played a large part in the design of the new United States currency. One among eighteen artists chosen after a nation-wide search to design new coins, his design was selected for the 2006 Colorado quarter. He and his wife, Janet, Father Robert Brungs' sister, have been longtime members of ITEST.*

# Contents

# Prayer for Those Studying Faith and Science

Most kind God, we gather here to listen, ponder and converse about you and the world we live in.

Like the blind reading Braille, the fingers of our minds feel their way trying to discern the contours of your glory arising from matter.

What really happened when you opened the hospitality of your great heart to make room for us?

How did the Spirit's energy weave worlds from your Word's love affair with matter?

Did your Word already have the Incarnation in mind as it shaped the worlds?

Did your Spirit delight in energizing a cosmic carnival of lights?

What do you have in mind when you say, "My Word does not return to me void…?"

Will we all be there, linked by love, beyond our wildest dreams?

Who are you, in whom we live and move and have our being?

We the fish, you the sea.

In your kindness, take the threads of our conversations and weave us wisdom, wide-eyed wisdom, that knowing that is salted with tears.

Keep our minds tucked into our hearts, so that we can speak truth that is tender.

Give us wisdom that we make real in our lives what our minds speak, and our hearts hope for.

Give us the wisdom that comes from wonder.

We ask this for the sake of your glory, in your Spirit who is active love, and in your Word which shapes beauty.

Amen.

September 21, 2007
Carla Mae Streeter, OP
Composed specially for the symposium

# Foreword

*Astronomy/Cosmology Breakthroughs and the God Question.* What an imposing title for a weekend ITEST symposium! A study of the "breakthroughs" alone could consume a month of weekends, but the God question too?

The members of the Board of Directors admit to some hesitancy in adopting this topic when Father Brungs suggested it in the fall of 2005. He had indicated that, although our primary interest lay in the area of the life sciences, we, as an institute, should prepare to lift our eyes from the God-given beauty of the Earth to the equally beautiful God-created wonders of the Heavens above. Sister Carla Mae Streeter, OP, provided the theological "piece" by adding "…and the God Question."

In studying the advances in science and technology we are asked to look beyond our sometimes self-centered concerns to the universe and the cosmos beyond. What or Who is it that guides us? Is it the Solar system held in such exquisite balance? What or Who in that wonderful ordered universe holds us human beings, in existence? In this instance, while the astronomers and cosmologists gaze upwards, the theologians and experimental scientists help to keep us anchored to earth.

In this volume we proudly present the papers of three essayists: Stephen Barr, PhD, cosmology, Guy Consolmagno, SJ, astronomy and Neyle Sollee, MD, interaction of science and faith. Responding from the theological and cultural viewpoints are: Rev. Dr. Steven Kuhl and Sebastian Mahfood, PhD, respectively.

Although the papers are a "must read" for anyone who is interested in planetary science, cosmology and theology, the discussion sessions reveal the "heart" of the symposium as the presenters and the participants engage in lively and sometimes heated (but always charitable) discussion and argument about the relationship of faith/theology to science and technology, multiverses, exo-planets, black holes, dark matter, nebulae, Anthropic coincidences and even the possibility of extraterrestrial beings. Would those "beings" need a Redeemer? The Incarnation? Would it be Jesus?

Further, how did the tasks accomplished through the Hubble telescope, the lunar landing, the walks in space engineered by NASA and other discoveries and breakthroughs speak to our relationship with the Deity? Are scientists truly aware of the beauty they discover as they observe the structure of a blood cell through the microscope or focus the lens on a telescope to view the countless stars in the Milky Way Galaxy? Are they moved to praise God for it?

In an urgent and passionate plea to the participants at the 2005 ITEST workshop, Father Robert Brungs, SJ asked, "Where are the Psalmists of the 21st century? Who in the scientific community sings of the beauty of Creation today, from the beauty of the universe, the comets, the planets, -- where are they? Why don't scientists look at what they are doing, and sing of the beauty of God?"

Let us see how scientists of faith at this symposium would respond if they were asked that question.

Stephen Barr, a 21st century psalmist and cosmologist answers: "In my talk I quoted Minucius Felix, (who saw) the classic argument of the orderliness of the universe pointing to a Law Giver. Now in the 21st century in fundamental physics we see the laws of nature so much more clearly and deeply. What astonishing, intricate, subtle, deep, profound mathematical structures! The world has an orderliness that goes far beyond what people of ancient times were able to see. They saw regularities in the Heavens; we see so much more now when we deal with theories of physics."

Neyle Sollee easily shares his understanding of the beauty and depth of the God of Creation. Here he reflects on bridging the gap that often exists between the layperson and the scientist. "I would want to be a person who reflects the wonder and mystery of all creation." Further, "At night looking through the telescope, my "field of view" can extend billions of light years away. Wonder and awe arise in me as I gaze on this (terrible) beauty. For me nature and grace, science and faith have always been in a harmonious relationship."

Brother Guy Consolmagno sings his praise of the Heavens: "What do I see in Creation, in Astronomy? First of all, beauty. Beauty is big to this God. Beauty is not something that happens by accident. Beauty is something that is there by design. I see phenomenal complexity that arises out of very simple principles… And I see stories. I can see from the cloud in Orion where stars are being formed to the planetary nebulae at the death of the stars with gas clouds bursting off and the gas and dust from those clouds then becoming more clouds, and more stars are being born… I see an evolution in the stars."

I think that Father Brungs has his answer.

Finally, we owe a debt of gratitude to Dr. Thomas P. Sheahen, our facilitator, who managed to make the running of the symposium look easy, We thank him too, not only for his managerial ability, but also for his contributions to the scientific side of the discussion. His ability to add commentary to the discussion drawing on his experience as a physicist and his knowledge of current developments in the field further added to the unity and coherence of the meeting.

I add an "extra" special thanks to Tom Sheahen for providing invaluable assistance in the editing of the transcripts of the proceedings. Without his help, this editor would have been hard pressed to find her way through the "morass" of mathematical equations, arcane formulae, and ancient Greek symbols so prevalent in the scientific field.

Borrowing the lines from Father Brungs at the end of the Foreword to the 2005 proceedings:

"I recommend the results to you all."

Marianne Postiglione, RSM
ITEST: Acting Director
May, 2008

# Astronomy/Cosmology Breakthroughs and the God Question

## Essays

*Proceedings of the ITEST Symposium - September, 2007*

# Planetary Science Breakthroughs and the God Question

**Brother Guy Consolmagno, SJ**
**Vatican Observatory**

Brother Guy Consolmagno, SJ was born in Detroit, Michigan. He earned under-graduate and masters' degrees from MIT, and a PhD in Planetary Science from the University of Arizona, was a researcher at Harvard and MIT, served in the US Peace Corps (Kenya), and taught university physics at Lafayette College before entering the Jesuits in 1989.

At the Vatican Observatory since 1993, his research explores connections between meteorites, asteroids and the evolution of small solar system bodies, observing Kui-per Belt comets with the Vatican's 1.8 meter telescope in Arizona, and curating the Vatican meteorite collection. Along with more than 100 scientific publications, he is the author of a number of books including *Turn Left at Orion* (with Dan Davis), *Worlds Apart: A Textbook in Planetary Sciences* (with Martha Schaefer), *The Way to the Dwelling of Light,* and *Brother Astronomer;* his latest book, *God's Mechanics*, will be published in October.

Dr. Consolmagno has served on the governing board of the Meteoritical Society and is presently chair of the Division for Planetary Sciences of the American Astronomi-cal Society. He is a past president of the International Astronomical Union, Com-mission 16 (Planets and Satellites) and current secretary of Division III (Planetary Systems sciences). He has held chairs as a visiting Jesuit scholar at St. Joseph's University and at Fordham University.

In the opening words of the Creed we claim to believe in a God who created heaven and earth. As astronomy expands our understanding of what is in creation and how it operates, it inevitably colors the ways we understand who that God is and how that God acts. A particularly significant challenge that astronomy gives to this creed is the way it redefines the meaning of "heaven and earth."

Today, I want to concentrate on how the branch of astronomy that has come to be named *planetary science* has provided ever new visions of what "earth" actually means. I am going to concentrate on three aspects: how understanding the motions of the planets has, over history, constrained our ideas of the universe; how the detailed exploration of our own solar system is bringing home in an emotional way the nature of other planets as real places and possible homes for life, ours or aliens'; and how the discovery of other planetary systems has given a new impetus to the concept of "other worlds."

**Early History**

When the writers of the creed talked about God creating the "earth" they were thinking of the physical universe in general. They assumed that the physical universe was equivalent to, and no more than, the earth they saw all around them. You look around and can see for yourself what the universe looks like. There is this flat disk of dirt and streams and lakes we call "here," the earth; and a sky overhead that makes a dome over this disk, that we call the "heavens." (Remember, in Romance languages, the word for sky is the same as the word for *heaven.)*

That's the basis of all ancient cosmologies; and so the first chapter of Genesis describes God creating such a sky, "a dome in the midst of the waters" that separates the "waters" above and below the land on which plants, animals, and people are eventually placed.

You can develop this picture – many ancient cultures did – by postulating all sorts of different heavens, layers of heaven, that line up with your understanding of the spiritual realm. Thus, last spring when I was speaking to a group of native American elders in northern Wisconsin about meteorites, rocks that fall out of the sky, they wanted to know: which sky?

You can see some stars in the nighttime sky that move among the other, fixed stars; these wandering stars are called *planets*. There are seven visible planets (if you include the sun and the moon); hence, seven levels of heaven that anyone can see for themselves.

The Pythagorean mathematician Eudoxus, about 350 BC, explained the observed motions of the planets by describing the universe as an elaborate system of interlocking transparent spheres whose axes of rotation pass through the Earth; by then, the Earth itself was long recognized as a sphere: probably the Pythagoreans had worked that out 150 years earlier. Aristotle (we're up to about 330 BC now) referred to the Eudoxus system in his geocentric cosmology. His physics was based on the idea that elements move so as to achieve their natural resting places, up or down, fire and air, water and earth… natural places that corresponded to "spheres of heaven" again. And Aristotle's work was the basis of most philosophical thought for the next 1500 years.

The Roman astronomer Ptolemy in the second century AD used the planetary observations by the Babylonians and Greeks to flesh out Aristotle's geocentric cosmology with mathematical rigor. He provided mathematical tools that worked, when it came to predicting the positions of the planets. Because they worked, for the next millennium philosophers accepted his cosmological premises as true. (The idea that if a system works for a particular case, then it must be true in general, is a common logical fallacy that continually plagues science.)

## Christianity and Cosmology

The Ptolemaic system was a far cry from the water-covered dome described in Genesis. St. Augustine noted this; writing *On the Literal Interpretation of Genesis* in the early 5th century he warned that "even a non-Christian knows something about the earth, the heavens, and the other elements of this world, about the motion and orbit of the stars and even their size and relative positions, about the predictable eclipses of the sun and moon, the cycles of the years and the seasons... and this knowledge he holds to as being certain from reason and experience. Now, it is a disgraceful and dangerous thing for a non-believer to hear a Christian, presumably giving the meaning of Holy Scripture, talking nonsense on these topics."

But this difference did not lead to a fifth-century crisis comparable to the Galileo affair. Instead, most theologians continued to see in this physical cosmology a reflection of the nonphysical universe. They assumed that the physical universe mirrors the spiritual realm, describing a "chain of creation" where the orbital "spheres" of the observed planets were assigned now to different ranks of angels. Beyond that, the perfect eternal circular motions of the planets were placed in contrast to the irregular and finite movements of objects on Earth. Earth itself stood not at the center of the universe, but at the bottom of the chain of creation, only one level removed from the levels of the Inferno. This was just one of many ways that theologians like Thomas Aquinas successfully reconciled Aristotle with Christian theology, doing their job so well that by the time of the Renaissance many people saw any challenge to Aristotle as a challenge to the principles of Christian theology itself. This helped give rise to the well-known problems between the church and the heliocentric viewpoint espoused most famously by Galileo.

But even the man who finally made the heliocentric model work, Johannes Kepler, adopted a personal cosmology that, like the medieval "Chain of Creation," drew connections between the physical and supernatural worlds. Recall that the original Copernican system of circular orbits still required small epicyclic motion of the sun about an average center point in order to match its observed position against the background stars, assuming the Earth and the planets moved in perfect circles. Seeing a parallel between light emitted from the sun falling on the Earth, and the Holy Spirit radiating from the Father onto the Son, Kepler argued against that epicylic motion, and replaced those circles and epicycles with elliptical planetary orbits. This allowed the sun to remain stationary at the center of the universe – as (he argued) would only be fitting for the physical analogue of God the Father.

The new physics of Isaac Newton fifty years later provided a viable replacement for Aristotle's system. It successfully reproduced Kepler's elliptical orbits by using physical laws that acted the same both on celestial bodies and objects as humble as an apple falling from a tree. The Earth and everything on it was no longer at the bottom of a chain of creation, but raised to a status equal to that of the other planets. Newton's physics showed that "Earth" was not in a unique place in the universe, favored or disfavored in contrast to the heavens.

It completed what had started with the heliocentric revolution: the death of the concept that the physical universe could be thought of as a parallel to the spiritual universe. And this, in turn, freed up science to look more carefully at the concept of "other worlds." The medievals had understood how thoughts of other worlds would shatter the sense that the physical world paralleled spiritual reality. If there were other worlds, would that mean there were other layers of other kinds of angels around each star? But they knew that to deny the possibility of other worlds denied the omnipotence of God.

The reality of other worlds has been understood, intellectually, since the enlightenment; indeed, we've had stories speculating about life on other planets since

Roman times. In the 1920s, the development of the airplane and radio made it feel reasonable that one could possibly travel to such places; this laid the groundwork for the new genre of science fiction, which mass-marketed this idea, albeit an idea still labeled as Amazing or Astounding. But it was only when we've actually been able to see the real planets in our solar system, close up, that this reality has come home to us at a gut, emotional level.

## Astronomical Observations

Let's remind ourselves of the reality that has been revealed for the first time to our generation: At Christmas of 1968, we first saw our own world as a planet, hanging over the alien horizon of the moon; subsequently, Astronauts' footprints were left on soil that never before felt human feet; since 2000, with the landing of *Spirit* and *Opportunity* on Mars, a robot presence on an alien desert placing human-caused tracks across the red sands to dunes and hills and a new sky, to a new alien horizon of rocks and cliffs waiting to be grabbed by human rock climbers and mapped by geologists; graced by sunsets both alien and yet oddly familiar, that inspire very familiar emotions in the human heart.... even when that human is a Martian.

And, following on a hundred years' speculation, in 1995 the first planets around other stars were detected.

I want to spend a few minutes here describing the science of how these planets are discovered, because I think there are some important lessons here for how science works, and doesn't work. First, it's important to keep in mind that we don't actually *see* these planets, but we know they are there only because we can measure how they affect the stars they orbit. We believe in them for a reason that sounds a lot like believing in God: we can't see them, but we deduce their presence by seeing how they act on things we *can* see.

The precision of optical measurements is truly exceptional. Our telescopes can measure to within an *arc-second*. As shown in Figure 1 on the next page, the circle of the sky can be divided into 360 degrees; a quarter of circle (a right angle) is 90 degrees; each degree is divided into 60 arc minutes; each minute is divided into 60 arc seconds. That's a very tiny angle, less than the width of a dime seen from two miles away.

When I was a kid I remember reading about a possible planet orbiting a small nearby star called Barnard's star. What some astronomers had done was mea-

6

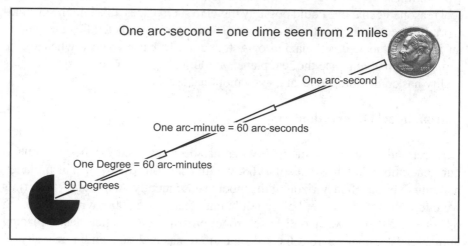

*Figure 1 - One arc-second*

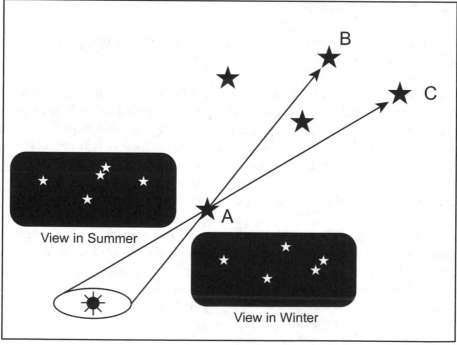

*Figure 2 - parallax view*

sure the position of that faint star relative to other stars on various photographic plates, taken over many years. They thought they saw the star wiggle back and forth as it moved past the other stars, as if there were a small, unseen mass of a Jupiter-sized planet going around it, pulling it back and forth. Other astronomers were skeptical; and it turns out the skeptics were right. The measurements reported in the 1960s have not been confirmed by other observers. The shifts in the star's position appear to be associated with slight changes in the telescope itself, during its regular maintenance over the years.

Barnard's Star is the second closest star system to us, less than six light years away, and so its motions compared to background stars are among the easiest to see. But it has lots of different motions. The star moves through the galaxy, in orbit around the galactic center: that's its "proper motion." In more detailed measurements, astronomers saw a back-and-forth wiggle around the path of its proper motion, but that's not the evidence for a planet out there. That wiggle had a period of one Earth year. We were seeing the *parallax* shift.

The concept of *parallax* is illustrated by Figure 2 on the opposing page. The star appears to move back and forth compared to more distant stars. However, this is actually caused by the Earth's own back-and-forth motion around our star. The motion is small, about an arc-second total. The blurring of the Barnard's star images were more than an arc second. So even to measure this Earth parallax, astronomers have to take the average of many, many images.

Now, hidden in amongst all these other motions, to find a planet you have to pull out an even smaller wiggle that only shows up over a much longer period of time. Think about it: to find something like Jupiter pulling on a star, back and forth, you have to observe over at least one orbit of the Jupiter-like planet. Given that Jupiter itself takes 12 Earth years to complete an orbit, you can see the difficulty: you would have to follow a star for 12, or better 24 or 36 years, to be sure you're seeing the same reflex motion over and over. (The Barnard Star measurements ran from 1938 until into the 1980s; and they were all for naught, so far as finding planets were concerned.)

Measuring the exact position of a star is hard to do – it really takes a spacecraft above the Earth's turbulent atmosphere to do that right. But there is another way to detect this tiny motion. Instead of measuring the back and forth motion of the star, we measure slight changes in its *speed* towards us and away from us, via the *Doppler Shift*, illustrated in Figure 3 shown on the next page. Astronomers observe how the wavelengths of certain emission lines are shifted blue, then red,

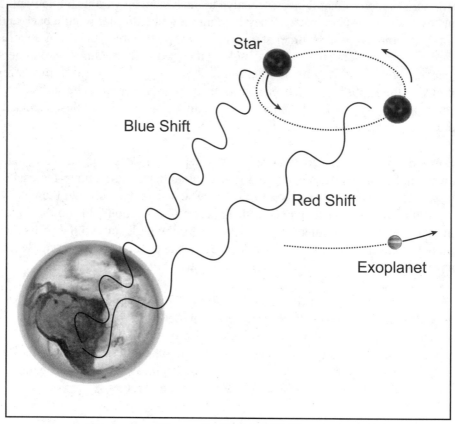

*Figure 3 - Doppler Shift*

then blue, as the planet pulls its star toward us, then away from us, then toward us again, over and over.

The bigger the mass of the planet, the more the star is tugged at; so measuring the amount of blue shift and red shift lets us measure the mass of the planet. And measuring how long it takes to shift back and forth tells us how long its year is; using Kepler's laws of orbits we can calculate from the length of its year how far from the star it orbits.

It's still a really hard measurement to make; only in the last ten years have our detectors become sensitive enough to detect such motion. Given that we figured Jupiter-sized planets would take decades to complete one orbit, no one expected to be able to report any planets for years to come.

But it turns out, we were pleasantly surprised. We found stars with big planets, Jupiter-sized or so, orbiting their stars in much shorter orbits than we expected – a matter of days, not years, in many cases.

Nowadays we are also finding planets by watching their star's light dim slightly as they cross the disk of their star, as seen from Earth. By measuring the depth of the dip we can calculate the physical size of the planet, and combine that with the mass to see if these planets are gas balls (like Jupiter) or somewhat denser ice balls (like Neptune) or – possibly – truly dense rock balls like our Earth. Indeed in a few cases we can even see how gases (their atmospheres), absorb the light from their stars, telling us what chemicals are present in those atmospheres. Yes, in some cases, we have found water.

Earlier in 2007, a team lead by Stéphane Udry of the Geneva Observatory announced the discovery of three planets around the red dwarf star Gliese-581, a star only 20 light years away from us. Apparently one of these planets is only about eight times the mass of Earth and about 50% bigger in radius. Orbiting close to its sun, its "year" is less than two weeks long; but because that star is so small and dim compared to ours, even at that close distance the temperatures on this planet will only range between zero and 40 ºC (averaging about 70 ºF). Room temperature. Water should be liquid there, perhaps covering its surface with oceans ripe for life.

Space telescopes optimized to search for planets, especially terrestrial planets, are being designed; the first are being built; a French prototype called COROT has already been launched, and found its first planets. A target of one of those missions is to study dense fields of stars such as in the constellation Cygnus. Instead of the 200 or so planetary systems that have been discovered so far, ten years from now we may know tens of thousands of systems that have planets... including, I repeat, Earth-sized terrestrial planets. This is "many worlds" with a vengeance.

**Life on Other Planets ?**

All these planets pose the ever increasing possibility of extra-terrestrial intelligence. Indeed, for the last twenty years there's been an intense (if so far unsuccessful) search for life outside of Earth. How does this challenge the assumptions underlying the traditional explanations of original sin and Christ's salvation?

This question has been debated for centuries. 200 years ago, the astronomer John Herschel saw life on other planets as the inevitable result of God's fecundity, while Thomas Paine mocked the idea of a Saviour who had to suffer and die, over and over again, on countless worlds.

If there are other planets suitable for life, if there is life on those planets, if that life is intelligent, if that life is in a free, self-aware, loving relationship with the Creator, if that life can communicate to us about their experience of that relationship... well, that's a lot of "ifs." If it's so, then certainly we could have a lot to talk to each other about. But if any of that chain of "ifs" turns out wrong, we'll never know. Yet even if it is never known, the very possibility of other planets raises those questions. I have my own ideas on this topic, and I suspect you do, too.

Meanwhile, something more fundamental is happening here. We are not only looking in a new way at the meaning of "heaven and earth"; we are also looking in a new way at the act of creation. Because all these new planetary systems have implications for the "how" of creation proceeds. New, not in the sense that we are seeing planets formed in some way different from "what the Bible says" but rather, new in that unlike the hundreds of years (going back to Immanuel Kant) of theorizing about "solar nebulas," we are actually *seeing* solar nebulas, solar systems in the act of being formed.

For generations everybody studying solar systems knew that rocky planets like Earth and Mars are found close to the Sun, while gas giants like Jupiter and Saturn were farther out; this was a fundamental starting point in every theory of how planets were formed. But now we have found hundreds of cases where gas giant planets orbit very close to their stars. Time to rethink our theories, right? Maybe; maybe not. Not surprisingly, more massive planets are easier to discover, and those are most of the ones we've seen so far. Have we found so many of them only because they are easy to find, or is the overwhelming number of such systems evidence that this is a fundamental characteristic true for most stars with planets? We still don't know. Science in itself never deals with certainties. Rather, we scientists are satisfied if we can come up with a theory that's merely consistent with what we think we've observed up to now.

**Advances in Understanding**

Another example of how science has advanced beyond the Enlightenment is our growing understanding of the essential role of stochastic – random – events such as giant impacts in the evolution of the Earth. The big debate in 19th century geology was between "catastrophic" versus "uniformitarian" views of nature. Did the Earth get shaped by sudden disasters, like the Biblical flood? Or were the hills and mountains shaped by slow, gradual processes no different from what we can see operating today, only occurring over enormously long periods of time?

By the time I started studying geology, everybody knew that "the present is the key to the past," that uniform events over a long period of time could explain everything we see in nature, and "catastrophism" was on the scrap heap of science... along with "epicycles" and "phlogisten."

But once we started looking at the surfaces of other planets, covered with craters, peppered and indeed at times shattered by impacts, it's turned out that both ideas are right; catastrophes, like giant impacts or sudden massive episodes of volcanism or mass extinctions, do happen. On a human time scale they are rare, but if you look over geologic time they occur all the time. Catastrophes occur uniformly. We learned that only by studying other planets, then applying what we learned there to our own planet.

The point is this: in some ways, the concept of a "scientific revolution" is very misleading. Yes, disruptions in our understanding do take place – catastrophically, as it were – and they happen all the time. But it's not that what we knew before is false, that "everything you know is wrong," and that we're finally so much smarter than we were in the middle ages, or in the 19th century, or ten years ago. What these advances tell us is that everything we thought we knew then, is still true, but in a different way than we understood it before. That's the way science works – not just natural science, but all kinds of *scientia* in the Latin sense of "knowledge." That's the way knowledge works.

The most important aspects of these challenges are not in the confrontation of new facts to old theories, religious or scientific. Rather, it is in how they reveal the unrecognized assumptions we have made in our previous understanding of heaven and earth, and by extension the assumptions we have made in our understanding of God as the creator of earth and heaven. It is both new, and familiar. What we once thought was the physical universe, earth, turns out to be only one tiny bit of it. What we once thought of as heaven, the stars and planets, turns out to be just a bigger part of "earth." What we now think of as heaven, let's call it the locus of the Beatific Vision, is not a location accessible to our telescopes; but whatever, wherever, whenever it is, it too is a creation of the same creator God we say we believe in at the very beginning of our credo.

*Figure 4 - Saturn seen with the Sun behind it.*

Our *scientia,* our knowledge, grows when we see the familiar from new angles. Figure 4 shows Saturn as seen from "behind" – seen with the Sun behind it. Even in this new view, the awe we feel is a familiar awe, the joy a familiar joy, the same that the Psalmist felt when he wrote that the heavens proclaim the glory of God. We find our center, our starting point, in old, familiar truths. Are you able to see the small white dot on the ring of light (at approximately the 7:00 o-clock position) surrounding the planet? That's the Earth.

*Francisco Muller poses a question*

*l to r: A. McGuire, Sr. Marcianne, C. Wesley*

# Anthropic Arguments, Multiverses, and Design Arguments: Future Prospects

**Stephen M. Barr**
**University of Delaware**

Stephen M. Barr is a theoretical particle physicist. He received his PhD from Princeton University in 1978 and went on to do postdoctoral work at the University of Pennsylvania. After holding research faculty positions at the University of Washington and Brookhaven National Laboratory he joined the faculty of the University of Delaware in 1987, where he is a professor in the Department of Physics and Astronomy and a member of its Bartol Research Institute. His physics research centers mainly on "grand unified theories" and the cosmology of the early universe. He has written over 120 research papers, as well as the article on Grand Unification for the Encyclopedia of Physics. He writes and lectures extensively on the relation of science and religion. Many of his articles and reviews have appeared in *First Things*, on whose editorial advisory board he serves. He has also written for *National Review, The Public Interest, The Weekly Standard, The National Catholic Bioethics Quarterly, Columbia Magazine*, and other publications. He is the author of *Modern Physics and Ancient Faith* (University of Notre Dame Press, 2003) and *A Student's Guide to Natural Science* (Intercollegiate Studies Institute, 2006). He is on the board of The Fellowship of Catholic Scholars. He lives in Newark, Delaware with his wife Kathleen and their five children.

In recent years there has been much discussion both in the popular press and among physicists of the so-called "Anthropic Principle." of the "fine-tuning" of the laws of physics for life, and of the possibility that there are many universes or that there is one universe that is really a "multiverse." In fact, in the last two or three years the discussions of these ideas within the world of fundamental physics have intensified and become at times quite heated. In this paper I will explain what these ideas are, what their relevance to religion might be, what reactions they have provoked among physicists, why these discussions have intensified recently, and whether future discoveries might shed light on these issues.

For a long time it has been noticed that the laws of nature appear in certain ways to be arranged, or even finely adjusted, to make life possible. For example, as long ago as 1802, the Anglican divine William Paley pointed out that if the gravitational force did not obey a so-called inverse square law (more precisely, if the gravitational force fell off as distance to the $-n$ power where n is an integer greater than 2), then the earth could not remain in a stable orbit around the sun, but would either plunge into the sun or fly off into space. Another example known for a long time is that water has many singular, in some cases almost unique, properties that make it able to function as the medium of life. In the twentieth century, as more has been learned of the structure of the laws of physics, a number of parameters that appear in those laws have been found to have only narrow ranges that would permit life. For example, if the strength of the so-called "strong force" that holds atomic nuclei together were different by even a few percent from what it is the consequences would have been catastrophic for the possibility of life. If it were a few percent weaker, it would be too weak to hold together the deuterium nucleus, a crucial stepping stone in the formation of all chemical elements except hydrogen. If it were a few percent stronger, it would allow the sun and similar stars to burn very rapidly by a new kind of nuclear fusion process, so that life would not have had time to evolve on earth or other planets.

The fact that the laws of physics have some feature that is just right for making the emergence of life possible is sometimes referred to as an "anthropic coincidence." There are several kinds. (a) There are parameters whose extreme smallness is necessary for life to exist. An example is the "cosmological constant" (denoted $\Lambda$), a parameter appearing in Einstein's theory of gravity, which must be smaller than about $10^{-120}$. Another example is the "spatial curvature" of the universe, which had to be extremely small near the time of the Big Bang. If these two parameters had not been extremely small, either the universe would have expanded ferociously fast, ripping galaxies, stars, and even atoms apart, or else it would have collapsed upon itself very soon after the Big Bang. (b) There are other parameters (or combinations of parameters) whose values must lie in a very narrow range for life to be possible, though they needn't be small. The strength of the strong force mentioned above is a commonly cited example. (c) There are certain integers (rather than continuous parameters) appearing in the laws of physics or characterizing the structure of the universe that must take particular values if life is to be possible. For example, under certain assumptions it can be argued that the number of space dimensions must be three for life to exist. (d) There are qualitative features of the laws of physics that seem necessary for life. Two examples are the quantum mechanical nature of the laws of physics and the fact that electromagnetic forces exist. Sometimes people say that the laws of nature are "fine-tuned" for life; but that terminology only fits anthropic coincidences of types (a) and (b).

It is fairly clear to most physicists who have examined the arguments that there really are some striking anthropic coincidences. Many people see in them evidence that the universe was designed for the purpose of giving rise to living beings, including highly complicated and intelligent living beings such as ourselves. The potential religious implications are obvious. However, they are not inescapable. Some of the physicists who have done the most to call attention to the anthropic coincidences do not see them as evidence for God, but are convinced that the "coincidences" have a natural rather than supernatural explanation.

More often than "anthropic coincidences." one hears the term "Anthropic Principle." It is a very unfortunate term for a number of reasons, not least because it is highly ambiguous. Some people use it merely to refer to the anthropic coincidences themselves, which is confusing. Others use it to refer to an asserted metaphysical principle according to which the universe must *necessarily* have the capacity to generate intelligent life — though it is never really explained where this principle comes from or why anyone should take it seriously. Others use it to refer to the rather jejune observation that if the laws of physics did not permit life we would not be here. Finally, others use "Anthropic Principle" to refer to a certain speculative hypothesis for explaining the anthropic coincidences in a naturalistic way. It is becoming increasingly common to call this speculative hypothesis the "multiverse" idea, which is less confusing and therefore to be preferred.

The multiverse idea is best explained by an analogy. We see that conditions on earth are in many ways "just right" for life. There is an abundance of water.

The mean temperature is not too high or too low, but lies in the range where water is liquid. The surface gravity is enough to retain an atmosphere, but not so large as to make the earth a "gas giant" like Jupiter. The presence of a large moon stabilizes the earth's rotational motion, allowing for moderate seasonal changes. What accounts for the "coincidence" that so many of the conditions for life are satisfied on earth? Undoubtedly, the fact that there are so many planets in the universe. Most of those planets are too cold, or too large, or have the wrong kind of atmosphere, or are for some other reason inhospitable. But with at least $10^{22}$ planets in the observable part of the universe, there are bound to be many that are "just right" for life — and only on such planets, of course, will life exist. So, the fact that there are many planets explains the otherwise strange "coincidence." If you buy enough lottery tickets, one is bound to pay off. The multiverse idea applies the same idea to universes — or rather to regions of the universe. We are asked to suppose that the universe is made up of many regions, or "domains." among which conditions vary so greatly that even the very laws of physics appear to be different from one domain to another. Deep down, all the domains would really have the same "fundamental laws." but those fundamental laws would manifest themselves in different ways in different places, so that in different domains different "effective laws" would prevail. For example, the strength of the strong force, the cosmological constant, the spatial curvature, and other quantities might vary from one domain to another. Even qualitative features could vary among domains. For example, there might be such a thing as electromagnetism in some domains, but not in others. Or there might be such particles as protons in some domains and not in others.

If the "multiverse" contained within it a sufficiently rich variety of domains, it might allow a natural explanation of most or even of all of the "anthropic coincidences." For example, if the strength of the strong force varies from domain to domain in such a way as to "scan" over all possible values, then *somewhere* in the multiverse it is bound to have the right value for life. So "anthropic explanations" can be made in radically different forms, a design/teleological form and a multiverse/naturalistic form. Many people point to anthropic coincidences as evidence of design and purpose in nature. But some of the scientists who advance "anthropic" explanations based on the multiverse idea see it as providing a naturalistic explanation of the anthropic coincidences and thereby *weakening* the case for God.

The multiverse scenario may sound far-fetched, but it really isn't. In the context of present day ideas in fundamental physics, it is a speculation that should be taken seriously. Two things are required for a multiverse: (1) a universe large enough that it can have a domain structure; and (2) fundamental laws that are able to manifest themselves in a wide variety of "effective laws."

The reason the universe has to be large to have a domain structure is that if domains were small we would have seen them. That is, we know from various observations that the laws of physics are the same to a high degree of accuracy throughout the whole part of the universe that is observable to us, which is to say to a distance of about 10 billion light-years. (The so-called "horizon" of 10 billion light-years is set by the fact that light or other signals from anything farther away would not have had the time to reach us since the Big Bang.) Therefore, a universe with a very large number of domains would have to be much larger, exponentially larger, than the present horizon. But there are very good reasons to believe that the universe is indeed so big. In particular, there are very powerful theoretical reasons to believe that something called "cosmological inflation" happened early in the history of the universe. According to this idea (without which it is very hard to account for certain facts), shortly after the Big Bang the universe went through a period of extremely rapid expansion, during which it increased in size by an exponentially large factor. If the idea of cosmological inflation is correct — and most theoretical cosmologists think it is — then the universe may indeed be big enough for the multiverse explanation of anthropic coincidences to work.

The second condition is that there must be different effective laws in different parts of the universe. That, too, is not implausible. How might it happen? Consider the analogy of ice, water, and steam. They are so different in their properties that they might even appear to be altogether different substances obeying different laws. But, a deeper investigation reveals that they are merely different forms — or, as the physicist would say, different "phases" — of the same substance. In each case the $H_2O$ molecules are satisfying the same basic equations of physics, but they satisfy those equations in different ways. Similarly, when one looks at certain theories of subatomic physics, one finds that the equations can be satisfied in different ways, giving rise to different phases of matter. And those different phases can be very different indeed: in different phases a force (such as the strong force) can have different strengths, or there can be different forces altogether, and there can even be different kinds of "elementary particles."

Just as in a single glass of ice-water, some parts are in the liquid phase and some in the solid phase, coexisting with each other, so in the same universe it is possible for different parts to be in different phases. Indeed, what phase each region of the universe ends up in depends on local conditions and *cannot* depend on what is happening in other regions that are so far away as to be out of touch (or, in the jargon of cosmology, "out of causal contact"). For example, parts of the universe that are beyond our "horizon" have no reason to be in the same phase as we are.

The idea of a multiverse is thus not intrinsically implausible. But that does not mean that we actually live in one, or that (if we do) it has a sufficiently rich variety to account for the anthropic coincidences. Whether we live in a multiverse is impossible to determine at present, and it is far from clear how we could ever determine it. For reasons already explained, we cannot look beyond our horizon to see whether there are domains out there with different effective laws. Thus a *direct* observational answer to the question is almost certainly forever beyond our reach. What might be possible eventually — though it is a very tall order — is to discover the truly fundamental laws of physics, establish that they are the correct ones by adequate laboratory tests, and then show by a mathematical analysis of those laws that they *require* the universe to be a multiverse. If all of that ever comes to pass, it will probably be far in the future.

What is the attitude of fundamental physicists toward these ideas? The dominant reaction of rank-and-file fundamental physicists a strong distaste, even a disgust, for the whole subject. This reaction is not entirely rational, but several reasons are offered by scientists who feel this way. In the first place, it is said that anthropic explanations are not truly scientific explanations at all, but rather divert people from looking for them. For example, one might explain the daily rising of the sun by saying that it makes life on earth possible. But if one were content with that as an explanation, one would never seek out the correct explanation of how the various bodies of the solar system move, how the sun was formed, and so forth. A statement that one often hears is that accepting anthropic explanations is "giving up." A second objection is that anthropic explanations are untestable and therefore not really science. This objection can be made both to the more teleological type of anthropic explanation ("the laws are this way in order to make life possible") and to the multiverse version ("we observe the laws to be this way because we are in a domain where life is possible").

Third, there is a deeply ingrained distrust of anything that looks at all like teleology. This is due partly to philosophical prejudice, and partly to historical experience. When science was done teleologically, as in the days when Aristotelianism reigned supreme, science made very little progress. It is a commonplace that the Scientific Revolution was made possible by the conscious rejection of teleology in favor of mechanism. Finally, there is the fact that anthropic explanations "smell of religion and Intelligent Design." as an eminent physicist put it in explaining his hostility to them, which he honestly admitted to be a visceral reaction and "not totally rational."

There is a lot of irony in the present situation. Most fundamental physicists reject anthropic explanations and do not wish even to discuss them, because they see them as teleological or religious or both. At the same time, some of the leading proponents of the possible utility of anthropic explanations are declared atheists and opponents of teleology. It is almost certain that there are anthropic coincidences, i.e. that the laws of physics at least *give the appearance* of being designed to make life possible. The only way of explaining that appearance in a naturalistic way is some version of the multiverse or many-universe idea. Thus, if one is an intelligent atheist, one should find the multiverse idea very attractive. That is presumably one reason why such strongly atheistic scientists as Steven Weinberg, Andrei Linde, and Max Tegmark are attracted to it. Nevertheless, most scientists who are atheists are led by their atheism to vilify anything "anthropic" in character. Weinberg sees the absurdity of this, and has explicitly defended the idea of the multiverse on atheistic grounds. Another irony has to do with the complaint of untestability. Of course, this is a familiar objection to belief in God. Now we see the same objection being raised against the multiverse idea. The multiverse idea should be attractive to atheists as the only way to make sense of some aspects of the physical universe without invoking God; but many of them are prevented from taking this idea seriously by the same positivistic reflexes that made them atheists to begin with.

I have mentioned several common objections of a philosophical sort raised by scientists to anthropic ideas. But there are also several standard *scientific* objections to the very idea of anthropic coincidences. One such objection, which has a certain amount of force, is that we don't know enough to say with certainty what is necessary for life to arise. When we say that the laws of physics must have a certain feature for life to arise that could simply be a failure of imagination on our part. For example, some anthropic arguments are based on the premise that life requires complex chemistry and therefore a multiplicity of chemical elements. That is part of the argument about the anthropic "tuning" of the strong force: if the strong force were slightly weaker, the nuclei of elements heavier than hydrogen would not be able to form; and with only hydrogen one cannot make life. However, it has been suggested that even with only the element hydrogen to work with, life of some sort might still be possible. Who really knows what kinds of strange life might exist elsewhere in the universe? Some have even suggested that life of some sort could exist inside the sun. While it is hard to exclude such wild possibilities rigorously, I don't think most scientists really take them very seriously. Scientists who have hopes of finding evidence of extraterrestrial life generally expect it to be based on carbon chemistry and to be found on the surfaces of planets having a significant amount of water. In any event, a number of the anthropic coincidences are based on very weak assumptions about what is needed for life. So, while absolute rigor in these matters may not be possible, some anthropic arguments can be made with a reasonable degree of confidence.

A second objection is that some of the anthropic coincidences may later be found to have conventional scientific explanations. For example, the extreme smallness of the spatial curvature of the universe shortly after the Big Bang, which is a commonly cited example of an anthropic "fine-tuning." is probably explained by the phenomenon of cosmological inflation. (A consequence of cosmological inflation is that it stretches the fabric of space out to be very flat, just as a balloon if inflated to very large size would have a very flat surface.) It seems quite likely that other features of the laws of physics or the structure of the universe that are required for life may be found to have conventional explanations as well. However, even if all the facts that are anthropically coincidental were found to have conventional explanations, it would not make the coincidences less coincidental. As Carr and Rees observed in a well-known review article on anthropic coincidences in *Nature* back in 1979:

"One day we have a more physical explanation for some of the relationships ... that now seem genuine coincidences. For example, the coincidence that $\alpha_G = (m_e/M_W)^8$, which is essential for [the synthesis of the elements], may eventually be subsumed as a consequence of some presently unformulated unified physical theory. However, even if all apparently anthropic coincidences could be explained in this way, it would still be remarkable that the relationships dictated by physical theory happened also to be those propitious for life."

In recent years several developments have caused many physicists to take both the anthropic coincidences and the multiverse idea more seriously. In 1987, Steven Weinberg proposed an anthropic explanation of the smallness of the cosmological constant. People had been searching for a conventional scientific explanation of this fact for decades. Indeed, the "cosmological constant problem" is widely considered to be the greatest unsolved problem in fundamental physics. Many ideas for solving it had been tried and failed. Weinberg noted that a cosmological constant much larger than the existing "experimental upper limit" would have prevented galaxies and other cosmic structure from forming, thus making life as we know it impossible. But on the other hand, he noted that there is no anthropic reason why the cosmological constant had to be any smaller than the existing upper limit. So, in a multiverse scenario, one would expect to find the cosmological constant to be nonzero and not too far below the existing limit. This was an interesting prediction, because most theorists at that time thought that the cosmological constant was probably exactly zero. (After all, it was known to be zero to more than 120 decimal places.) Lo and behold, in 1998 evidence was found that most of the energy in the universe is in a form now called "dark energy," which behaves very similarly to and is very likely to be a non-zero cosmological constant. Of course, that does not prove that the multiverse explanation of the cosmological constant is correct. But it could be seen as a striking, even if not a precise, prediction. Both this fact, and the enormous reputation of Weinberg (a Nobel laureate, and perhaps the leading theoretical particle physicist of his generation) made it more respectable to talk about and even publish papers on anthropic coincidences.

I have a personal story to tell in this regard. In 1998, three collaborators (V. Agrawal, J.F. Donoghue, and D. Seckel) and I submitted a paper to the leading journal *Physical Review*, in which we proposed an anthropic explanation of another great unsolved problem in fundamental physics, namely why a certain parameter called the "weak scale" has the very small value $10^{-17}$. Although neither of the two anonymous referees gave our paper a negative report, the editor took the highly unusual step of vetoing the paper, explaining in a lengthy letter that the whole idea of anthropic explanations was profoundly "unscientific." At the same time, however, we had submitted a highly condensed account of our work to the much more prestigious journal *Physical Review Letters*, and it was accepted for publication by them, having gotten two quite positive referee reports, one of them by none other than Steven Weinberg, as we later found out. This gave the editor of *Physical Review* little choice but to reverse himself. Our "unscientific" paper, after receiving only a few citations per year until 2005, has been cited in the scientific literature about forty times in the last two years alone, many of the citations being by top physicists, such as Steven Weinberg, Frank Wilczek, Martin Rees, Andrei Linde, Alexander Vilenkin, Savas Dimopoulos, Nima Arkani-Hamed, and Michael Douglas. When a student and I submitted a sequel to that 1998 paper to *Physical Review* a few months ago it was accepted for publication without a ripple. So, the climate of opinion has changed.

Even more important than Weinberg's work on the cosmological constant, the situation in string theory has given impetus to anthropic thinking. String theory was developed in the early 1970s, but people did not realize its great potential as a fundamental theory until the so-called "superstring revolution" of 1984. One of the striking features of superstring theory is that it appeared to have no "free parameters." Almost all physics theories have parameters in them whose values are not prescribed by the logic of the theory itself, but must be determined by experimental measurement. For example, in our present theory of elementary particles, called the Standard Model, there are 26 such parameters, including such things as the mass of the electron and the masses of the various types of "quarks." The theory does not predict the values of those parameters, one has to measure them. However, superstring theory seemed to contain no such free parameters, and so it was expected that it would be able (in theory anyway, if not necessarily in practice) to predict *everything* about the behavior of elementary particles from first principles.

That heady dream seems to have been dashed by an unpleasant reality. While superstring theory has no free parameters of the conventional sort, it seems to have many "ground states" — basically like the "phases" we discussed earlier. As $H_2O$ can appear as ice, water, and steam, so superstrings can appear in a multiplicity of guises — and not just a few phases like $H_2O$, but rather in an exponentially large number of ground states, some recent estimates put the number at $10^{500}$, i.e. 1 with five-hundred zeroes after it. In effect, having such ground states is equivalent to introducing parameters into the theory: each phase corresponds to certain physical quantities taking particular values. Physicists have come to call the vast set or space of ground states of superstring theory "the landscape." Which ground state or phase in this landscape is the correct one? Many physicists hope that it will turn out that some physical principle selects a particular ground state as favored over the others, just as at certain temperatures and pressures $H_2O$ is physically forced to be ice rather than water or steam. However, some theorists are beginning to doubt that that is the case. And if the theory turns out to have a vast number of equally good ground states, it forces one to consider the possibility that different parts of the universe have ended up in different ground states — precisely the multiverse scenario. In other words, the "landscape" of superstring theory may very well imply that the universe is a multiverse.

What this would mean is that far from explaining quantitatively and from first principles all the fundamental features of the physical universe in a conventional way, as was dreamt of at first, superstring theory may actually predict relatively little in the long run. Many fundamental quantities — like the electron mass, say, or the strength of the strong force — may actually "scan." i.e. vary from domain to domain. Many features of the world we see may turn out just to be features of our particular domain and only explicable by anthropic considerations. For many physicists, the dream is turning into a nightmare. What had seemed to be the most predictive theory imaginable may be the least predictive theory imaginable.

Some theorists who had turned up their noses at anthropic explanations and the multiverse have now concluded that the combination of string theory and cosmological inflation almost require them. That is the message of the book *The Cosmic Landscape: String Theory and the Illusion of Intelligent Design*, by Leonard Susskind, a leading theoretical particle physicist.

What does the future of theoretical physics hold, and will it allow us to decide some of these questions? One must distinguish the short-term and the long-term future. And to understand what might be learned in the short-term and long-term one needs to understand what is mean by a "scale" of physics. Every kind of basic physical process has an associated scale that sets the characteristic sizes, times, and energies of those processes. For example, there is an atomic scale that determines the size of atoms (about $10^{-8}$ cm) and the typical energies involved in (chemical) reactions among atoms. There is also a nuclear scale that determines the size of atomic nuclei (about $10^{-13}$ cm) and the typical energies involved in nuclear reactions. To study a particular realm of phenomena one needs devices that can probe to the relevant scale, i.e. to the relevant sizes and energies. (Smaller sizes turn out to correspond to larger energies, for reasons having to do with the principles of quantum mechanics. It is because nuclei are much smaller than atoms that nuclear energies are much larger than chemical energies. To probe smaller scales requires larger energy, which means bigger and more expensive machines. Atoms can be probed using table-top devices, whereas studying subatomic processes requires increasing huge accelerators, or in popular parlance "atom smashers"). Every time a new scale of basic physics has been probed, new kinds of phenomena, structures and particles have been seen. When atomic scales could first be probed, physicists discovered, of course, atoms as well as the electrons which make up their outer parts. When nuclear scales could be reached, physicists discovered nuclei and the protons and neutrons of which they are composed.

The Standard Model tells us that there is another scale of physics called the "weak scale." named that because it is connected with the so-called "weak force." In the next few years, a new and very powerful machine called the LHC (the Large Hadron Collider) will reach down to the weak scale — distances of about $10^{-17}$cm (10,000 times smaller than a nucleus). It is expected that a rich lode of new phenomena and new kinds of particles will be discovered. As I noted earlier, there is a big unsolved problem connected with this weak scale, namely why the associated energies are so small, or equivalently why the associated distances are so large. The distance $10^{-17}$ cm is tiny compared to an atom or nucleus, but it is huge compared to a certain fundamental distance called the Planck length, which is about $10^{-33}$ cm. Theorists have had a hard time explaining why the weak scale of length is so different from the Planck length. All conventional ideas for solving the problem of the weak scale, i.e. explaining its size, involve the existence of new kinds of particles that should be discovered at the LHC.

However, there is a radical possibility, namely that the size of the weak scale is explained anthropically rather than by conventional physics ideas. (That was the proposal of Agrawal, Barr, Donoghue, and Seckel in 1998.) If that is so, there may be no new kinds of particles and phenomena to find at the LHC. To particle physicists such as myself, that is a very disturbing possibility — it would spell the doom of our field. Most particle physicists, including myself, don't think this is very likely. I would be willing to give long odds that the LHC will find many new things. But what if it doesn't find anything new, i.e. nothing beyond what the present Standard Model says it should find (namely the so-called Higgs particle)? In that case, it would strongly suggest that the anthropic explanation of the weak scale is correct. On the other hand, if — as I expect — lots of new phenomena are found at the weak scale by the LHC, it will not necessarily say that the anthropic explanation is wrong. The anthropic explanation of the weak scale does not *require* new physics at the weak scale (as other explanations do), but is not incompatible with it either.

The short-term future (the next ten to twenty years) is certain to be extremely interesting. The longer term future may be very dull. The reason is that the answers to many of the deepest questions of physics most probably lie not at the soon-to-be-probed weak scale, but at the perhaps-impossible-to-probe Planck scale. It is easily proved that it is utterly impossible to build a machine that comes anywhere near being able to probe the Planck scale directly. It can only be studied, if at all, by very indirect means. One possibility is that so many pieces of the puzzle may be put in place with what is learned at the LHC, that physicists will be able to guess the whole picture without much further help from experiment. That is a long shot. Another possibility is that certain very elusive phenomena may be observed (such as the long-sought "proton decay") that will give enough indirect clues to what is happening at the Planck-scale to allow the whole puzzle to be solved. Again, this would require quite a bit of good luck. A third possibility is that someone will be able to "solve" superstring theory (or some other "theory of everything") mathematically and show that it "postdicts" things about the world that we already know and that the Standard Model is unable to account for. That seems like an even longer shot.

Unfortunately, at present there are no solid grounds for optimism that we will arrive at the ultimate theory of physics and be able to show convincingly from experiment that it is the right one.

That would leave us in a very awkward position: On the one hand, if we do live in a multiverse, we certainly cannot see other domains directly: they are outside our "horizon." On the other hand, if we do not find the ultimate theory or find it but are unable to confirm it experimentally, we shall not be able to prove by a theoretical argument that we live in a multiverse either. The history of science is full of surprises, but it doesn't seem likely, at the moment, that science will ever be able to answer definitely whether the multiverse idea is correct.

I do expect that we will find conventional explanations for some of the anthropically coincidental features of the world, just as we probably have found the explanation of the small spatial curvature of the universe. However, even if we found conventional explanations for all of them, it would not make them less anthropically coincidental, as Carr and Rees pointed out in the passage I quoted above. There would still be the question of why so many of the features of the universe are "just right" for life. And that question would have two possible answers: a teleological/religious one and the multiverse one. There would remain what the philosopher Peter van Inwagen calls a Mexican standoff between the two answers.

However, in my view, even if we discover somehow that we do live in a multiverse, I think that an argument for a cosmic purpose that includes life can still be made on the basis of the anthropic coincidences. What the anthropic coincidences teach is that life would not be likely to arise in a universe with just any old laws of physics. The laws of physics must in one way or another be very *special*. They may be special in that various parameters are finely tuned to just the right values. Or they may be special in giving rise to a multiverse. *For not any old set of laws will give rise to a multiverse either*; a multiverse itself requires a number of rather strong conditions to hold. In other words, *that we live in a multiverse could itself be seen as an anthropic coincidence.*

In conclusion, we may never know for sure whether we live in a multiverse, but it may not matter much from the point of view of natural theology whether we do. That the universe is life-bearing is not something that we can take for granted; rather it should be seen as a very remarkable fact, a fact that can be seen, even without faith, as pointing to God.

*Stephen Barr delivers his address*

*Students soaking up the wisdom: Kathryn Anthony, Victor Poole*

# From Microscopes to Telescopes

**Arthur Neyle Sollee, MD**

A. Neyle Sollee, MD is a physician with many interests. Twenty years ago, he retired from a successful practice of hospital pathologist and seriously studied physics and astronomy. His experience of the beauty of mathematics was the driving force along with his ever deepening desire to learn more about the world around him. He built a house and observatory in south central Colorado and spent many hours reading, praying, doing astrophotography, research with NASA and becoming friends with a group of Catholic monks. *Ora et labora* was his motto for fifteen years. But after fifteen years of this life, he decided to come down from the mountain and re-enter the city to resume the practice of hospital pathology and to share his many blessings.

Sollee is currently Assistant Professor of Surgical Pathology in the Department of Pathology and Laboratory Medicine at Methodist University Hospital, in Memphis, Tennessee.

The micro-world and the macro-world have always fascinated me. I have built two astronomical observatories. The first one in Memphis Tennessee in 1980 and the second in Crestone Colorado at the base of fourteen thousand foot Sangre de Cristo Mountains (www.sangreobservatory.com). It is here in this mountain town that I spent fifteen years engaged in *ora et labora* and this last observatory has been recently donated to Rainwater Observatory in French Camp Mississippi (www.rainwaterobservatory.org). Coming down from the mountain in 2002 I got retrained and took up again the practice of medicine (pathology). I entered the common life of ordinary women and men.

Observing God's creation from the telescope and microscope always reminds me of the organic connection between the book of nature and the book of scripture. Our conference today features two professional scientists, one a particle physicist and the other an astronomer. Having always been an amateur (amour, one who does something for the love of it) astronomer and a student of general relativity and theology, it seems my task today is to share some thoughts and reflections on the interaction of science and faith. The so-called "God problem" is nothing more that an example of the disjunction of the faith and reason. My day job is a hospital general pathologist. Most of my day is spent rendering pathological diagnosis on biopsy specimens sent from the operating room or doctors offices. I am sort of a "doctor's doctor." Under the microscope the small becomes very large. All of nature's beauty and deadliness come under my microscopic field of view. At night looking through the telescope my "field of view" can extend billions of light years away. Wonder and awe arise in me as I gaze on this (terrible) beauty. For me nature and grace, science and faith have always been in a harmonious relationship. Truth cannot contradict truth. It seems such is not the case for many in this so-called modern or post-modern age.

Having the unity of all creation as my underlying theme, I would like to share with you and propose a possible unifying world-view that may re-establish a certain "great chain of being" for our time – a unity between God's physical creation (physical cosmology and biological evolution) and our Christian faith – *this is the cruciform kenotic universe model.*

This basic theme of a kenotic and cruciform universe comes from Nancy Murphy and George Ellis and Holmes Rolston. The book *The Moral Nature of the Universe* (Murphy and Ellis) and the journal *Zygon* article by Holmes Rolston, (vol. 29, no. 2 June 1994), "Does Nature Need Redemption," serve as a foundation for my presentation today.

Science, physical and biological, attempts to explain the created world from the vantage point of secondary causes. But causes that relate to purpose or final end are the purview of philosophy, metaphysics and religion. The denial of any meaning or purpose (atheistic materialism) is a growing and pernicious sickness of our times. I am reminded of Stephen Weinberg's often quoted statement, "the more I study the universe, the more meaningless it becomes." I wonder if Weinberg has a special equation that shows "meaning?"

Ethics and morals are areas that empirical science is not able to offer us any solutions. It is blatantly absurd to look to the empirical sciences for answers to moral and ethical questions. Pray tell, how will Heisenberg's uncertainty principle get us out of Iraq or multiverses change the human heart from hatred to tolerance (how about just human friendship?). So my reflections today concern the human person and her soul, from the anthropic principles to the anthropos – the human being and the human condition.

To me faith and science have always had an integral connection – the mind and the heart for me have always resonated harmoniously. This type of solidarity is usually referred to in theological terms as the relationship between nature and grace. This theological connection has not always been very healthy in theological writings as Karl Rahner states in his book, *Nature and Grace: Dilemmas in the Modern Church*[1], that the neo-scholastic presentation of nature and grace was a two compartment construct, both of which lightly interacted. So we see a fragmented human condition nowadays mainly going back to the Middle Ages and on to Descartes where the mind and the heart started their disunion. This has come down to us culturally as the great division between nature and grace.

Science is a language. It's the great language of nature. But it's not a language that describes the whole world. For the everyday person, science mainly touches them through technology. With the advent of cloning the biological science will shortly press upon the common person in a new way. I recall the many fine papers by George Ellis on the topic of "physics and the real world" and the "illusion of a purely rational life." These articles remind us that the empirical sciences are just part of the "real" world of joy and sorrow, purpose and meaning. All people seem to have some basic faith in their particular world-view.

This split between faith and science or faith and reason is well known and is exemplified in a contemporary cosmologist named Sean Carroll. Obviously a

---

1 Karl Rahner, *Nature and Grace: Dilemmas in the Modern Church* (New York: Sheed & Ward, 1964)

brilliant man in the empirical sciences but outspoken atheist. He apparently can't stomach all these cosmological coincidences of fine-tuning that smack of a creator so he uses terms such as "Is Our Universe Natural?" (http://arxiv.org/abs/hep-th/0512148) and "the preposterous universe" (http://preposterousuniverse.com/). Carroll also uses the phrase "coincidence scandal" which refers to the apparent fine-tuning in which the density parameter of matter is of the same magnitude as the density parameter of the vacuum energy.

An interesting comment on this "unnaturalness" is given by physicist Richard Conn Henry (Journal of Scientific Exploration, Issue 20-4) http://henry.pha.jhu.edu/rch.html: Physicists have for some time been grappling with the fact that the Universe that is observed, by both physicists and astronomers, does not look natural: it looks, forgive me, intelligently designed. In this insight … Sean Carroll describes the situation nicely, and he also paints a clear picture of what are currently being considered as escapes from what is, to many, an unpalatable situation…. but I must mention that in my own opinion, the whole problem was solved in 1925 with the discovery of quantum mechanics. In the conventional majority, Copenhagen interpretation of quantum mechanics, all that is real is the observations themselves plus, of course, your perceiving mind (which is the one thing that you know is real). Now, physics has never even suggested what an observation is, or what *mind* is. Yet these are the only things that actually exist, according to that same physics! The observations, our minds discover, have the character of numbers, and in practice what physics is, is the successful search for relationships among these numbers. At least, it keeps us busy! So, to resolve the big question, all you need to do is to decide whether your mind (on which the observations persist in intruding) is natural, or is unnatural: for that is the Universe you need to decide whether or not that Universe is, as Pope Benedict XVI recently asserted it to be, an intelligent project. Good luck!

The origins of modern secularism and atheism are discussed in detail in Michael J. Buckley's S.J. books, *At the Origin of Modern Atheism* and *Denying and Disclosing God, The Ambiguous Progress of Modern Atheism*. Buckley's thesis is that starting with Descartes, theologians have "bracketed" their religious faith until it has become almost nonexistent as a meaningful theological topic. As Pope Benedict XVI recently said "Christianity is the faith of Creative Reason not Unreason," and it has been this "self-limiting of Western reason" that is at the root of much of modern atheism and "according to the thought of St. Thomas Aquinas, human reason, to say it as such, 'breathes,' that is, it moves on a wide-open horizon in which it can experience the best of itself. Nonetheless, when man limits himself to think only of material and experimental objects, he closes himself to the questions of life, about himself and about God, impoverishing himself." -- Benedict XVI, Feast of Thomas Aquinas, January 28, 2007

Buckley states in the preface of *Denying and Disclosing God* (page xv), "...the lesson that emerges is that one cannot – in an effort to justify, found, or confirm assertions of the reality of God – bracket or excise religious evidence and religious consciousness and the interpersonal that marks authentic religious life and experience. Religion must be allowed to bear the full complement of constituents that Baron von Hugel (*The Mystical Element of Religion as studied in Saint Catherine of Genoa and her Friends* (London:J.M.Dent & Co.,1909, 50-82) has argued as essential: the intuitional, emotional, and volitional; the speculative and rational; the institutional, historical, and traditional. Excise any of these, and the account of the religious affirmations is seriously deficient."

The Catholic theologians at the time of Descartes for the most part handed over questions concerning the existence of God to the philosophical arena. The philosophers accepted this charge and ran with it! Descartes dedicated his greatest work, his *Meditations of First Philosophy* to the faculty of theology at Paris (~ 1641) and said: "I have always been of the opinion that the two questions that have to do either with God or with the soul were the chief among those to be demonstrated by the power of philosophy rather than be that of theology." So Descartes is saying to the theologians that now it is his responsibility to demonstrate the existence of God and not theirs. (*Denying and Disclosing God*, p.33)

## *Models of the Universe*

### A. The Medieval Model

C.S. Lewis describes the medieval world-view in his last book, *The Discarded Image*[2]. Lewis describes it as, "...the medieval synthesis itself, the whole organization of their theology, science and history into a single, complex, harmonious mental Model of the Universe." This model was intelligible to the layman and appealed to his imagination and emotion and is seen comparable to the Summa of Aquinas and Dante's Divine Comedy. This esthetic Model was geocentric but man was seen more on the periphery. As Lewis says, "the Medieval Model is, if we may use the word anthropoperipheral, we are creatures of the Margin." (p. 58, *The Discarded Image*) This "discarded image" or "great chain of being" held central place in the mind of western man for centuries. (www.nature.com/nature/journal/v435/n7041/full/435429a.html)

---

2 C.S. Lewis, *The Discarded Image* (Cambridge University Press: Cambridge, 1964)

The Copernican revolution will certainly strike a deadly blow to this medieval world-view. The Copernican revolution understood as not only Copernicus' work but the subsequent development that he gave momentum too. Catholic priest and cosmologist Michael Heller describes these developing areas as: "(1) unification of the 'earthly physics' and the 'physics of heaven', (2) dehierarchization of the Universe, (3) geometrization and infinitization of space, (4) mathematization of science, (5) its mechanization, and (6) increasing of the role of controlled experimentation in science." (*Creative Tension*, p.41)

With Galileo and Newton we now have a method of dialogue with nature using the language of mathematics. Thus some would say, began the separation of man, the separation of methods of science from the methods of religion. After Galileo the entire medieval conception of a hierarchical structure of the world crumbled. Galileo's work was published in Italy in 1610 and spread quickly throughout the European continent. In 1611 the English poet John Dunne wrote:[3]

> The new Philosophy calls all in doubt,
> The Elements of fire is quite put out;
> The Sun is lost, and th'earth, and no man's wit
> Can well direct him where to look for it...
> 'Tis all in pieces, all coherence gone;
> All just supply, and all Relation;
> Prince, Subject, Father, Son, are things forgot ...

## B. The Cruciform and Kenotic Model of the Universe

This world-model is based upon Nancy Murphy and George Ellis' book, *The Moral Nature of the Universe* and on an article by Holmes Rolston in the journal Zygon (vol.29, no.2, June 1994), *Does Nature Need to be Redeemed?* This view of the Universe struck me as a possible way to approach the "problem of God" and a way to think about uniting the "book of nature" and the "book of scripture." Murphy and Ellis reflect on all the deep questions of existence. What is the true meaning and purpose of human life? Where did the created universe come from? Why is the universe law-like? Life shows us, that the world we live in is filled with violence, pain and suffering. I believe that this model can give some "meaning" to our every-day life, a life modeled after Jesus Christ. The biblical source of the word kenosis or emptying is the beautiful Christological hymn in Philippians 2:5-11 where Jesus is given to us as the archetype of self-emptying

---

3 John Dunne, *An Anatomie of the World: First Anniversary,* A.L.Clements, ed. (New York: W.W.Norton & Co., 1992)

love and reveals to us that His crucifixion and death reflects aspects of the very nature of God. One empties oneself so as to be filled (*pleroma*) with the transforming grace of God. One dies and empties oneself of self-love so as to be filled (*kenosis/pleroma*) with the transforming grace of God. Grace perfects nature. To enter into this transforming energy of God the individuals have to give their assent (fiat) to cooperate with grace and this is a dynamic on-going conversion (*metanoia*).

This assumption of a moral purpose in the creation can help explain the anthropic features of the universe and seems to place two constraints on the Universe: the first is the *law-like nature* of the universe and the second the possibility of individual *non-coercive free choice or free will*. To some cosmologists the mathematical laws and the moral code of conduct of the cosmos are imprinted into the very fabric of nature (Heller, Ellis, Penrose) and this order and rationality reflecting the mind of the Creator. The intelligibility of the universe is surely a *vestigae Dei*, a footprint of God. (Bonaventure's *Iterarium mentis in Deum*)

The physical laws of the universe have allowed for the emergence of biological complexity, so that intelligent beings are able to react and have the ability to freely choose between "light and darkness," good and evil. This free choice will always be constrained by various factors such as personal genetics, psychology, and one's cultural milieu. We cannot judge our neighbor given this complex dimension of the human person. I feel that is the main reason that Christ said: "Do not judge, least you be judged."

This notion of kenosis may help us develop a deeper Christian worldview of the Universe we live in. God has created and sustains this universe ("the whole she-bang") so that we human beings will have the opportunity to make a free, non-coercive choice to open ourselves to the transforming power of God. In Garrigou-Legrange's *The Three Ages of the Spiritual Life*, he describes the growth and development of the *spiritual organism*. He like so many spiritual theologians insist that the normal development of the human person consists in the life-long transformation with the eventual goal of transformation in Christ (divinization, *theosis*) and that *this life is normative for all Christians* or as Thomas Merton says in, *New Seeds of Contemplation*, "the Christian should have a contemplative orientation."

Ellis and Murphy show that in this model of a kenotic universe, there should be certain requirements and assumptions, such as: 1) a providential universe, 2) a God who is hidden and silent, and 3) possibility of divine revelation.

We see in nature the impartial operation of the laws of physics, chemistry and biology. This world presents all people with the freedom to choose. Jesus in the Gospels hides His power as He confronted the temptation in the desert. He refrained from turning stones into bread ("Tell these stones to become bread" Matt 4:3) so the olive branch of material comfort (promises, rewards, and bribes) would not sway people to follow Him. *Jesus gives us a radical model of non-coercion.* Our choice of "yes" awaits His graced invitation (He stands knocking at the door).

One of the most striking aspects of God's creation is His apparent hiddenness and silence. If God's presence was "out in front" so to speak, then a free choice would not be genuine. There are of course many hints and footprints of God's presence as we have seen. An act of faith is always needed to start on the road to injecting life into this spiritual organism.

The cruciform aspect of creation is laid out beautifully by Holmes Rolston's article *Does Nature Need To Be Redeemed?* With your permission, I would like to quote from this article:[4]

"The Earth is a divine creation and scene of providence. The whole natural history is somehow contained in God, God's doing, and that includes even suffering, which, if it is difficult to say simply that it is immediately from God, is not ultimately outside of God's plan and redemptive control. God absorbs suffering and transforms it into goodness. There is ample preparation for this conviction in Judaism, but it reaches its apex in the crucifixion and resurrection of a suffering Messiah, who produces life out of death in his followers. But we must be careful here. It is not simply the experience of divine design, of architectural perfection, that has generated the Christian hypothesis of God. Experiences of the power of survival, of new life rising out of the old, of the transformative character of suffering, of good resurrected out of evil, are even more forcefully those for which the theory of God has come to provide the most plausible hypothesis.

Christianity seeks to draw the harshness of nature into the concept of God, as it seeks by a doctrine of providence to draw all affliction into the divine will. This requires penetrating backward from a climaxing cross and resurrection to see how this is so. Nature is intelligible. Life forms are logical systems. *But nature is also cruciform.* The world is not a paradise of hedonistic ease, but a theater where life is learned and earned by labor, a drama where even the evils drive us

---

4 Holmes Rolston, *Does Nature Need To Be Redeemed* (Blackwell: London, 1994)

to make sense of things. Life is advanced not only by thought and action, but also by suffering, not only by logic but also by pathos.

The Greek word is pathos, "suffering," and there are pathologies in nature, such as the diseases of parasitism. But pathology is only part of the disvalue; even in health there is suffering. Life is indisputably prolific; it is just as indisputably pathetic, almost as if its logic were pathos, as if the whole of sentient nature were pathological. "Horribly cruel!" exclaimed Darwin. This pathetic element in nature is seen in faith to be at the deepest logical level the pathos in God. God is not in a simple way the Benevolent Architect, but is rather the *Suffering Redeemer*. The whole of the earthen metabolism needs to be understood as having this character. The God met in physics as the divine wellspring from which matter-energy bubbles up, as the upslope epistemic force, is in biology the suffering and resurrecting power that redeems life out of chaos. The point is not to paint the world as better or worse than it actually is in the interests of a religious doctrine but to see into the depths of what is taking place, what is inspiring the course of natural history, and to demand for this an adequate explanation. The secret of life is seen now to lie not so much in the heredity molecules, not so much in natural selection and the survival of the fittest, not so much in life's informational, cybernetic learning. *The secret of life is that it is a passion play.* Things perish in tragedy. The religions knew that full well, before biology arose to reconfirm it. But things perish with a passing over in which the sacrificed individual also flows in the river of life. Each of the suffering creatures is delivered over as an innocent sacrificed to preserve a line, a blood sacrifice perishing that others may live. We have a kind of "slaughter of the innocents," a nonmoral, naturalistic harbinger of the slaughter of the innocents at the birth of the Christ, all perhaps vignettes hinting of the innocent lamb slain from the foundation of the world. They share the labor of the divinity. In their lives, beautiful, tragic, and perpetually incomplete, they speak for God; they prophesy as they participate in the divine pathos. All have "borne our griefs and carried our sorrows."

Rolston is known as "the father of environmental ethics," for his defense of intrinsic value in nature and of caring for creation.

So in summary, the disunity between the "book of nature" and the "book of scripture" can be seen as a pathological division between faith and reason, nature and grace. This fracture of man's mind and spirit can be traced to the "bracketing" or artificial self-limiting of reason starting around the time of Descartes. The one constant symptom of this diseased state is such phraseology such as "the problem of God," or "the God question." For a thorough discussion of this "problem," the encyclical letter, *Fides et Ratio* (Faith and Reason) of John Paul II can be enlightening.

An evolutionary model of the emergence of material and biological complexity has been presented as a continual growth and development in the biological and spiritual realms. We called this model the "The Cruciform and Kenotic Model of the Universe." We come from the Source and we return to it through the saving power of Christ. This 'vital dust' has evolved into a conscious creature that can in some mysterious and wonderful way participate in the great Mystery.

*Steve Kuhl delivers his formal response*

*Greg Pouch and Ben Abell*

# Astronomy/Cosmology Breakthroughs and the God Question

# Session 1

*Proceedings of the ITEST Symposium - September, 2007*

44

**Stephen Barr:** I'm not actually going to read my talk so it doesn't really matter that I left my copy at home. If you have a copy of my talk, I might want to borrow it. I was asked to talk about breakthroughs in Cosmology and the God question. I am not strictly speaking, a cosmologist. I am a theoretical particle physicist. But the goal of particle physics is to figure out: What are the fundamental constituents of matter? What are the fundamental forces of nature by which these particles interact with each other? What are the fundamental mathematical laws which govern these particles and their forces?

Cosmology is the branch of physics which is concerned with the beginnings of the universe, and how the universe unfolded, and the structure of the universe on a large scale. Now these two branches of physics are very closely tied to each other. New ideas about what the fundamental particles forces were had a strong impact on ideas about how the universe unfolded and developed; and vice versa. Observations about cosmology fed back into theories of particle physics!

So, most theoretical particle physicists actually do some research in cosmology — Particle cosmology as it is called. About 10 – 20 percent of my own research actually has to do with cosmology. So I guess to some extent I'm a cosmologist. Also, I've been asked to talk about the "God question" in relation to cosmology. How do cosmology and physics, for example, relate to the Theology question and that question of God? There are a number of topics I could have talked about, and I'd be happy to talk about them in later sessions or another time. One topic is the Big Bang. Was it the beginning of the universe? Did the universe have a beginning? Questions like that. Time: what does modern physics tell us about the nature of Time? What might that have to do with various recent discussions among theologians about God's relationship to time? Does God change? Does God have a future? — and so on.

Now for the question of Design: whether what we learned in physics has anything to say about the old question of whether the universe is designed, whether indeed there is an intelligent designer. But instead of talking about those, I thought it would be interesting perhaps to talk about "*Anthropic coincidences.*"

*Anthropic coincidences* refer to features (or purported features) of the fundamental laws of physics that make life possible in our universe. People say that there are various features of the laws of physics, that the laws of physics seem to have been arranged and even in some cases fine-tuned in such a way as to make life possible in our universe. This obviously has potential theological implications, and people have made the argument that this points directly to the fact that the universe was created with the purpose of having life, in particular, human life.

I've also been asked to talk about something having to do with "breakthroughs" and I thought that anthropic coincidences would be a good topic because there have been some recent developments in particle physics which have sharpened the debate over the whole "Anthropic coincidences" question. It is anticipated that in the next 3 to 10 years there are going to be huge breakthroughs in particle physics, and these may shed light on the topic of Anthropic coincidences.

I like the word "breakthrough" and I'm glad that the ITEST staff chose that word when they were planning this symposium. I echo what Brother Guy said last night about the word "breakthroughs" in preference to the word "revolution." I think it's better in most instances not to talk about revolutions in science but breakthroughs. The word revolution gives you the idea that scientists had some ideas and they discovered that those ideas were just all wrong and they threw them out in the trash heap and replaced them with spanking new ideas. That is not how things generally work in science.

What you have are theories which are based on insights into nature. And what usually happens in breakthroughs is not that those insights are all thought to be wrong, but that they are supplemented by further deeper insights, which indeed sometimes qualify or modify the older insights; but usually the older insights are still found to have validity. It's really a building process – the new developments build upon the old ones.

I also want to say something about the phrase "fundamental laws." We talk about Anthropic coincidences as features or aspects of the fundamental laws that seem designed, arranged or fine-tuned to make life possible. What do we mean by "fundamental?" Well, the way science works is that you start discovering some laws of nature and then later people discover that these laws actually rest upon, follow from or are consequences of some deeper more encompassing laws. So for example, Kepler discovered these beautiful laws of planetary motion, and Galileo discovered the law of falling bodies , but Newton, decades later showed that there were deeper more fundamental, more encompassing laws from which Kepler's and Galileo's laws follow. And later Newton's laws of gravity (he had laws of gravity and mechanics) were shown to follow from yet deeper laws: Einstein's theory of gravity — general relativity. Many people suspect today that Einstein's theory of gravity rests on something yet more fundamental involving *super strings*, although that is still rather speculative.

The same thing happens in electricity, for example, in the 1700s people discovered separate laws of electricity, and laws of magnetism. In the 1860s they were all found to be parts of a deeper more fundamental theory: Maxwell's *theory of electromagnetism*. In the 1970s that theory was shown to be part of a yet deeper theory called the *electro-weak* theory. Thus, in science we don't build "up"; we sort of "build down." There is a layer of scientific theory and that layer is resting on a deeper foundation. You dig down to find that foundation, and then dig farther and find layer after layer. So the building of physics builds from the first floor down to basement after basement, and we haven't yet gotten to the deepest level — which might be *super strings*.

So there is a penetration of layer after layer of physical theory. What is exciting (and this is where the imminent breakthrough is likely to happen) is that people in the field of particle physics anticipate that we are just about to break through to a deeper level of theory in the next few years. A very large machine called the *Large Hadron Collider* is about to start operations, and we hope to learn about the next layer of theory, which is associated with the *"weak scale."* Of the four fundamental forces of nature, one is called the *weak force*. We expect to learn a lot about the weak force when we break through to this new layer. What's interesting here is that it may tell us something about this whole question of Anthropic coincidences.

As I said, Anthropic coincidences are certain features of the laws of physics which seem to make life possible. Some of these are gross qualities, for example, the law that nature has certain kinds of particles. The laws of physics have specified that there are certain kinds of particles – electrons, protons, neutrons, for example. What kind of particles are there in the laws? That makes a big difference. If we didn't have electrons, we wouldn't be able to have atoms, and we make living things out of atoms. So it is important that there be particles with certain kinds of properties. We certainly need electrons, protons and neutrons. As for some of the more exotic particles, it is not clear if they play much of a role in the existence of living things— we just don't yet know.

What kind of forces are there? There are four forces that we know about, as I mentioned. – *gravity, electromagnetism,* the *strong force* and the *weak force*. Each of these have peculiarities and properties which are important to life.

Gravity of course plays a very important role; it keeps us stuck to the earth; without gravity we'd all float off into space. Gravity is responsible for the stars and planets forming. Gravity plays many roles in how the universe is assembled. Likewise, electromagnetism plays a dominant role in how atoms interact with each other.

Another feature of the laws of physics is the fact that physics is *"quantum"* in nature – with basic principles from *quantum mechanics*. Regarding the gross qualitative features: there are certain kinds of particles and forces defining quantum mechanics. That's very important because (it can be argued that) if the world were not quantum mechanical, or if the laws of physics were "classical," that would have very severe consequences; and the universe would be radically different from the way it is, and very likely wouldn't be able to have life anything like the life that we know.

There are also quantitative features which are often referred to as 'fine tuning." If I have two charged particles – which attract or repel each other electrically, how strong do they attract or repel each other? How strong is that electrical force? It turns out that it is important how strong that force is. It shouldn't be too strong or too weak; otherwise that would have deleterious consequences — as far as the possibility of life is concerned.

Another important point is: how strong is the *strong force* between two protons. I've explained in my written version that if the strong force between protons and neutrons were just a little bit stronger, it would have disastrous consequences. Probably stars like the sun would burn so fast there wouldn't be time for life to evolve on the planets. Whereas if the force were a little weaker, that would prevent certain kinds of nuclear reactions from taking place. But it is important both for how stars burn, and how elements of the periodic table are manufactured. It turns out that some of these quantitative features apparently have to be adjusted just right in order to have life.

You may ask, "Are there Anthropic coincidences?" Is it really true to say that the laws of physics have to be just so in order to have life? I think most physicists who have thought about this would say "yes." Some people say there are only a few Anthropic coincidences; Steven Weinberg, for example. There may be only a couple of things that must be just right in order to have life. But probably more people who have looked into this and are interested in this would say that there are quite a few Anthropic coincidences — there may be dozens of them. Thus it is pretty safe to say, that "yes there are Anthropic coincidences." The question is, what do they mean?

At first glance they provide a slam-dunk argument for the existence of God who designed the world in order to have living beings in it. That's at first glance. But it's not so simple, because there is another way to explain why there are these coincidental features of the laws of physics.

That is the idea called the "*Multiverse*." I'll use an analogy to explain that idea. The Earth (and here I defer to Brother Guy, since it is not my field) has many features that seem to make it just right for life. It's not too hot; if it were too hot, it would boil away all the water. If it were too cold, everything would freeze. We can't have too strong or too weak gravity, we want to have a certain chemical composition in the atmosphere, we want to have liquid water; there are all sorts of things. So there are properties of Earth that make it a good habitat for life.

You can imagine things would have been different if Earth had been covered with a thick cloud cover so we didn't even know there were other stars or planets. We knew all modern physics but not that there were other stars or planets. Someone might say, "Look at the things on Earth; temperature is just right, gravity is just right, it clearly proves that God created this planet just to make it possible for us to be here." And you can imagine some scientist saying, "Wait a minute, I have a theory. That is not the way things are. Actually there are vast numbers of planets out there beyond the clouds; you just can't see them.—many billions of planets. Some of those planets have strong gravity and some have weak gravity; different chemical compositions; some have water and some don't. Almost every possibility is realized on some planet – and if there are enough planets, some of them are bound to have the right conditions for life. This is called the *Goldilocks* idea. Some are too hot; some are too cold; but there could be some that are just right."

That in fact is what we arrived at thus far. There are probably at least in the order of $10^{22}$ planets out there, more or less, and they do span a wide variety of conditions. There are some hot, some cold, and so on. That would cut the lights out of the idea that things on Earth were adjusted by God just so we could be here. The key for this many-worlds alternative explanation to work, of course, was that first you had to have many planets. You have to have conditions varying among those planets and you need all of the supposedly anthropically important features to vary. It wouldn't be enough if all the planets had different temperatures, but they all had liquid water, the right gravity, whatever. Because then you would only explain why the temperature on Earth was the right temperature for life. To explain all the Anthropic coincidences you have to have all of the coincidental features varying among the planets. You then have a rich smorgasbord of possibilities realized on these planets.

The Multiverse idea extends this common sense idea — but it extends it from planets to regions of the universe. What it says is: if you go far away to places in the universe that are so far away from us that you can't observe them, one might find that they had different laws of physics, or at least that the laws of physics appeared different. For example in our part of the universe there are electrons. But in a distant part there may be different particles, maybe there are no electrons. In our part of the universe the electric force has a certain strength, but at distant parts it may have other strengths — and so on.

If that were true, if the laws of physics in different parts of the universe realized a rich smorgasbord of possibilities, then you might be able to explain all these Anthropic coincidences in a purely naturalistic way without invoking God. So, if I were an atheist, an intelligent one, I would embrace the Multiverse idea with enthusiasm because, really, the only way to get around the question of the existence of God based on Anthropic coincidence is some version of the Multiverse. I cannot think of any other way of getting out of this argument for God from Anthropic coincidences.

Atheists ought to embrace the multiverse idea. As we will see, they don't embrace it, for some strange reasons.

What are the attitudes of various people toward these Anthropic ideas? Well, religious people, and most of them who seem to write about this subject, seem to warmly embrace the idea that there are Anthropic coincidences. Which is good! But many of them blithely dismiss the whole Multiverse idea, often with ridicule. They say, that's just some desperate idea cooked up by atheists to avoid the inevitable and obvious conclusion that God has arranged things on Earth for us to be here.

They are wrong! The idea of Multiverse is not cooked up just for anti-religious reasons. No doubt, some of the people who propagate multiverse are animated by anti-religious feeling, but that's not the only reason why the Multiverse idea is discussed. There are respectable scientific grounds for taking the idea of the Multiverse seriously. It has to be taken seriously as a possibility. It may well be right.

In my paper, in the context of contemporary particle physics theories, there are strong reasons to believe that the universe is very much larger than we can see, and that in distant places the laws of physics may look very different — may manifest themselves in very different ways. There are strong reasons to believe that. Whether there will be a rich smorgasbord of possibilities among those domains is a big question, but it is not an absurd idea that the universe has a Multiverse structure. It may not, but it is not an implausible idea at all.

Another thing that some religious people say is, "Well, OK, but it is untestable." They like to turn the guns of their enemies against them. Positivists and atheists have long argued this way against religion: "Well you can't test your `existence of God' in the laboratory." So they turn the guns against the Atheists and say the Multiverse idea is all smoke and mirrors and not testable. Well, may that's true. But it is kind of irrelevant because, if you're trying to make an argument for the existence of God based on Anthropic coincidences, the burden of proof lies on you to show that the Anthropic coincidences cannot be explained in any other plausible way.

Even if we can't ever prove the Multiverse, the fact that it might be, (and it is not implausible) is something that has to be reckoned with. So, if religious people are mocking or dismissing out of hand the idea of Multiverse, they should cut it out. It doesn't do them credit.

Now what about the attitudes of scientists? Some of the more intelligent scientists (some of the more astute ones, like Steven Weinberg, Leonard Susskind and others) understand what's at stake here. They realize that the only way to avoid a religious interpretation of the Anthropic coincidences is with a Multiverse idea – and not only for that reason. They are very much interested in the Multiverse idea and would favor a consideration of that idea. The rank and file, interestingly enough – (I was among the "average Joe" particle theorists) – tend to have intense hostility to the whole idea of the Multiverse and the whole idea of Anthropic coincidences – just the whole subject galls them to no end.

I was at a physics conference in the Summer of 2006 in California. There were a number of particle physicists there, and in the evening (as sort of entertainment) they had a panel discussion/debate between four eminent particle physicists. One was Burton Richter, a Nobel prize winning experimentalist; the other three were top theorists: Frank Wilczek, Leonard Susskind and Andrei Linde – all heavy hitters. It was an interesting debate. The three theorists (interestingly enough) all had a rather favorable attitude towards Anthropic explanations: they said that most things about the laws of nature we will understand by conventional kinds of scientific explanations, but probably there are certain things about the laws of nature which have an Anthropic explanation. – or a Multiverse type of explanation. The experimentalist disagreed vehemently with the other three, saying "This is all nonsense; it is not science at all, it is untestable. Why don't you get back to real science instead of all this speculative nonsense?"

I personally found that the arguments of the three theorists were very persuasive. They literally mopped the floor with Richter, and they won hands down as far as the strength of their arguments went. However, there is a deep division among scientists on this whole question. Talking with some of my friends (scientists who are atheists) at the conference, I learned that they didn't want to hear anything about "Anthropic coincidences" and the Multiverse. As I say, that's kind of paradoxical, and I think it shows that they are not very astute (they're smart but not astute). If they are atheists, the Anthropic coincidences are probably there whether they like it or not. There are striking examples of Anthropic coincidences, and even some scientists who are atheists agree that it is striking that certain aspects and laws of physics are just right (even fine-tuned) to make life. You can't get away from that. So they ought to be interested in these ideas and they ought to go for the Multiverse idea. Yet, a lot of the rank and file in the scientific community don't want to hear anything of it. If you use the word "Anthropic" in their presence they act disgusted.

Part of this is a strong anti-teleological reflex many scientists have, for understandable reasons. They know that modern science got on- track when people stopped looking for teleological explanations for things and started examining the mechanisms. Someone said to me, "If we had been content with explaining why the sun comes up in the east every day, obviously it comes up in the east for our benefit , to warm the Earth and make life possible. That's why the sun comes up. If people had been content with that explanation, they would not have looked for explanations of why the heavenly bodies move the way they do, how stars formed and why they shine and that kind of thing. So, we would have not done science."

That's what a lot of scientists say if you even think about Anthropic explanations: you are abandoning the path of science to say that things are the way they are because of Anthropic explanations; you are giving up on science. Others say that Anthropic explanations are not really explanations — that is not how science explains things. Many others will say "well, that smells like religion" — as one famous scientist of my acquaintance said to me. This division of attitude among scientists is sometimes rather heated among scientists.

In spite of the strong resistance of most scientists to this whole subject, the fact is that more and more people are talking about the fine tunings of the laws of nature and Anthropic coincidences and Multiverses . There are a couple of things that forced these subjects on the attention of scientists despite themselves. One major player is Steven Weinberg, who is a militant atheist, a pugnacious atheist propagandist (but not as bad as Dawkins). He also happens to be one of the greatest particle physicists of his generation. Weinberg wrote a paper in 1987 in which he proposed a Multiverse version of an Anthropic explanation of a crucial parameter of the laws of physics that is called the *cosmological constant* (the energy density of empty space). When Weinberg did that, it sort of opened the door and made it more respectable for people to talk about these things. Of course the Multiverse idea, to repeat, can be used as a sort of anti-religious argument.

Another set of things have happened: In the 1980s the idea of inflation was proposed – the idea that the universe expanded. Soon after the big bang, the universe went through a fantastically huge expansion in size very rapidly, and therefore the universe is probably vastly bigger than can be seen through the most powerful telescopes. Our telescopes show only a tiny, tiny patch of a much vaster universe. That opens the door to the possibility that the distant parts of the universe we can't see might have laws of physics that appear very different.

Even in relatively narrow old-fashioned theories of physics, like particle physics theories and *grand unified theories*, this condition happens: if you had a big universe, and different parts of the universe end up being in different phases, the laws of physics could be different. But recently in *Super string theory* (which many people hope is the ultimate theory of all physical phenomena), what's happened is that people have become aware that *Super String theory* has too many possible solutions. The equations can have vast numbers of different *ground states,* for example, $10^{500}$ of them, or even more. That, combined with the theory that the universe is very big suggests that the $10^{500}$ different kinds of physics will be seen in different parts of the universe. It almost forces you to believe in a Multiverse. Leonard Susskind, for example, is convinced that *Super String Theory* plus *inflation* almost compels you to believe in the Multiverse. So that's another reason why these ideas are now taken more seriously the last two or three years.

What do we learn from all this? A philosopher friend of mine from Notre Dame says that there is a Mexican Standoff. On the one hand there are Anthropic coincidences which some people say point to the existence of God who arranged things this way. On the other people disagree with that, for reasons which I've discussed here this morning, saying "it is rather a Multiverse and therefore things are this way."

How do we decide who's right? It's difficult because a lot of it depends on whether in fact we *are* in a Multiverse; and if we are in a Multiverse, is there a rich enough set of possibilities realized in these different parts of the universe to explain all the Anthropic coincidences in a naturalistic way? Those are going to be very very tough questions to answer. First of all, there is the obvious fact that we are not ever going to directly see those other parts of the universe. They are way beyond our "*horizon*." They are so far away that we can't see them even with the most powerful telescope. So we can't by direct observation look and see if we are in a Multiverse. It's possible we may theoretically conclude that we are in a Multiverse, that is, not by direct observation, but we may infer it very indirectly. For example, we can imagine that some day we can get our hands on the ultimate theory of physics, we'll be able to do enough laboratory tests to convince ourselves that this ultimate theory of physics is the big enchilada, the whole ball of wax. Someone will be able to solve the equations of those theories and see what kind of universe it leads to and show that it necessarily leads to a Multiverse. That could happen. But I would not hold my breath because it is a tall order. I hope it happens that we get the ultimate theory in our hands, the ultimate theory of physics, but I'm slightly pessimistic, and there are a lot of grounds to worry that we never will get that far. So we may never know whether we live in a Multiverse or not.

My own view is that that doesn't matter that much from a theological point of view. Even if somehow we find that we live in a Multiverse, if we find that all the Anthropic coincidences can be naturalistically explained by this Multiverse, I still think one can make a decent argument for the existence of God where one can argue that this points to the existence of God.

My thought is this: What the Anthropic coincidences highlight, what they underline and show us, is that not any old universe is going to have life. Not any old laws of physics will lead to a universe with life. Particle theorists spend their lives making up possible theories, possible laws of physics. We hope to come up with laws of physics that turn out to be the next step, the next most fundamental theory. So we cook up possible laws of physics for a living. Now what the Anthropic coincidences show us is that if you sat down and cooked up large numbers of possible universes (possible laws of physics), most of them are going to be sterile. Most of them will not have life. The Laws of Physics have to be special that way. That's important. If you tell me that you live in a Multiverse, within the universe (which is vast) with different regions having very different phenomena in them, different particles, different forces —that itself is saying it is a very special kind of universe. A Multiverse is a very special kind of universe. Most laws of physics that you might imagine right now don't lead to a Multiverse. One way or another, in order to have life in a universe, you have to have very special laws of physics. I think that is theologically significant. That is a little sign post pointing that this universe came from some source that had it in mind that there should be life.

**Sheahen:** We have asked Rev. Dr. Steven Kuhl and Dr. Sebastian Mahfood to make a formal response to the essayists. Dr. Kuhl will analyze the three papers from the theological viewpoint and Dr. Mahfood will concentrate on the philosophical and scientific aspects of the papers.

*l to r: G. Consolmagno, N. Sollee, S. Barr*

*Sebastian Mahfood responds to a question*

# Which God Question? A Response To The Essayists

**Steven C. Kuhl**
**Cardinal Stritch University**

The Rev. Dr. Steven C. Kuhl is a pastor in the Evangelical Lutheran Church in America (since 1984) and an Associate Professor of Historical Theology at Cardinal Stritch University in Milwaukee, WI. He holds a BS and an MS in Aerospace Engineering from the University of Minnesota, an M.Div. degree from Christ Seminary-Seminex, and a PhD in Systematic Theology from the Lutheran School of Theology in Chicago. He has presented papers at two previous ITEST Conferences entitled "Darwin's Dangerous Idea...and St. Paul's" (1997 Proceedings) and "The Cross-Purposes of God in the Science and Politics of Food" (1994 Proceedings). Heavily involved in the Ecumenical scene in Milwaukee, Dr. Kuhl represents the Greater Milwaukee Synod of the ELCA on the Unity and Relations Committee of the Wisconsin Council of Churches and on LARCSWORC (Lutheran-Anglican-Roman Catholic Spirituality and Worship Committee). He has served congregations in Chicago, IL and Mukwonago, WI and was an Associate Professor of Historical Theology and Ecumenical Relations from 2002-2006 at St. Francis Seminary of the Archdiocese of Milwaukee.

1. I want to begin by thanking our three keynote presenters for anchoring us in the topic and especially for their willingness to send their unpolished papers to me so that I might have a little more time to read and reflect on them. Being a perfectionist myself, I know first hand how anxiety producing it can be to let your thoughts into the public before you yourself are finished shaping them. So thanks for your generosity in that regard.

### Which God Question? The Existence Question or the Soteriological Question

2. What I don't see in any of the papers is a wrestling with the "meaning," ambiguity, or intent of the conference theme as stated: The God Question: Cosmology and Astronomy. So I am going to take some time to do that here. First, what is the topic? Is the topic "the God question [as asked in] cosmology and astronomy; or is it "the God question [as answered by] cosmology and astronomy? More importantly, what do we mean by the "God question?" Is the definite article "the" misleading?" Might there not be several kinds of God questions, questions that different disciplines may or may not be competent methodologically or instrumentally either to ask into clarity or to answer with any degree of confidence? The conference title, as I read it, explicitly evokes only two disciplines by name, Cosmology and Astronomy. Theology is only implicitly implied because the other two are being called upon to talk about theology's central focus of concern, God and God's relation to the world.

3. Having said that, from our three presenters, it seems that the "God question" as they understand it has to do with "whether God exists" and the "God problem," as they like to call it, is a matter of demonstrating God's existence on some rational, scientific grounds. This is certainly the "God Question" that often appears in the popular press. Neyle Sollee alone attempts to address this "God Question" (or "God problem") from a theological perspective, and I commend him for that. But, unfortunately, he does so by way of what seems to me to be a rather a-critical presentation of the Nature-Grace perspective of Thomas Aquinas (specifically *Summa Theologica* I.2.1-3), particularly, the strong teleological dimension of Aquinas' thought. I call his presentation "a-critical" because it ignores the vast philosophical and theological work since Hume and Kant that has credibly, in my judgment, relegated much of that interesting (teleological) aspect of Aquinas' thought and method to the category of the history of ideas. [For example, in his presentation, Sollee elucidated this tradition by way of the metaphor that Astronomy beholds the "finger prints" of God throughout the cosmos. But does it? Does Astronomy really give such obvious proof of God's

existence? Isn't Sollee really describing a pre-existing faith in the existence of God that is being read into the data, not the existence of God being read out of the data? This illustration might help clarify my point. When detectives go to a crime scheme they certainly see evidence of a disturbance. That's obvious. But does that constitute evidence of who did it? No. For *that* they need evidence of the criminal *himself*; they need finger prints, for example. And the "good thief" leaves no such evidence behind. That, I submit, is the way the biblical God works in the world. In general, God the creator leaves no finger prints of himself in his handiwork. What we know of him comes by way of "revelation," self-disclosure (usually in the form of proclamation), not investigation. God is far more elusive than the rationalist tradition imagines; and for various reasons that will be discussed more below.][1] To be sure, the hope of such a "rational proof" for the existence of God does still abound in the popular human imagination: Creation Science and Intelligent Design Theory, for example, are built on it, as are, perhaps, some interpretations of the so-called anthropic principle. Nevertheless, I think that such a hope is both illusory and unfaithful to the Christian view of God as incomprehensible: ungraspable and above the reach of human reason.[2]

4. Therefore, the question of demonstrating the existence of God, I submit, is not the "God question" that Christian Theology (biblically indicated and traditionally carried out, at least, pre-Scholasticism) has traditionally claimed competency to answer. Indeed, the nature of God's "existence" as understood in Christian theology is such that it cannot be proved in rational fashion; and it is the paradoxical burden of Christian theology to expound that fact in as reasonable way as possible. This epistemological limit is *not* meant to be a stop-gap, but the starting-point for *another* very practical "God question," what I will call the "soteriological question." Unfortunately, the "existence question" has often been a great distraction from the "soteriological question" which, to the best of my knowledge, is the one theological question to which Christian Theology claims a unique competency. That question, to borrow language from this Sunday's text (Luke 16:1-13) in the Revised Common Lection, goes something like this: how do we give an adequate accounting to God for our (mis)management of this, God's cosmos? That is the "God problem" Christian theology knows something about. From the perspective of Christian Theology, to focus too doggedly (or dogmatically) on the question of demonstrating God's existence as a prerequisite for any other question about God turns the "existence question" into, either, a ploy at self-justification or self-delusion: Self-justification because if the answer is "no," then, there is no God to render an account to, only ourselves (still, no small matter); or self-delusion because if the answer is "yes," then, religious people tend to make the presumptuous leap that by means of their very religios-

ity, they are able to make an adequate accounting of their stewardship. Indeed, to focus too dogmatically on the existence of God distracts also from the historical Event of Jesus Christ as God's own, gracious answer to the soteriological God question, which is the one thing Christian Theology claims unique competency in. But more on all this later. By the way, and I hope we can also talk about this more later, this soteriological God question (and answer) is not all together missing from Aquinas' theological vision. (See, for example, *ST* I.1.1 "the Nature and Extent of Sacred Doctrine" and *ST* III.49, "The Effects of Christ's Passion"). If Christians want to use Aquinas as a source of theological imagination (as increasingly not only Roman Catholics, but also some Protestants have[3]), they would do well to focus, not on Aquinas the Aristotelian Philosopher, but on Aquinas the biblical, Christian Theologian, taking their cues from the recent Aquinas studies influenced by M-D Chenu and J-P Torrell.

**Cosmology and Creation**

4. What about Cosmology or Astronomy? I submit that like Theology, they too lack the competency to answer "Yes" or "No" the Question of God's existence—and to presume so, does a great disservice to them also. Therefore, we must also ask what we mean by "cosmology" and "astronomy" as disciplines of study and the nature of their objects and competencies? To my mind, the object, scope and methods of Astronomy as a "scientific" discovery discipline are well defined within the grasp of human reason. It seeks to understand observable celestial phenomenon outside the earth's atmosphere. But the object, scope and methods of the discipline of "cosmology" are not so clear. As *The Encyclopedia of Philosophy* states, the term stands for a "family of related inquiries, all in some sense concerned with the world at large" of which "two main subgroups may be distinguished: those belonging to philosophy and those belonging to science." Whatever light cosmologists in the room can shed on this distinction would be helpful to me.

5. As I understand the term "cosmology," it was first coined in 1728 by the German Rationalist Philosopher Christian von Wolff in his *Discourse on Philosophy in General.* (Wolff is the bridge figure between Leibniz and Kant in the history of philosophy.) Cosmology was a catchall word meant to ask questions and seek understanding about, not the various "pieces" that make up the world, but the "world as a whole." Cosmology, as Wolff presented it, entails identifying the root, elemental, building-block "substance" of the world ("simples," as he called them) and, in a rather pedantic fashion, follow how they come together, observing and explaining the emerging collectives in mathematical, theoretical

terms. The cosmos is in some sense the sum of its parts. Therefore, "cosmology" emerged not strictly as a "scientific" discipline or concept, but as a philosophical or hermeneutical one, as philosopher's, under the materialistic impulse of Modernity, strove to update its work, relating its traditional concerns to the findings of modern science, in this case, Newtonian physics and its mathematical explanation of things, which it took as providing proof for a kind of "unified theory" of the physical world (and by analogy of its metaphysics, its sub- or super-structure, depending on ones outlook) that is thoroughly rational and comprehendible to the human mind.

6. Although I'm not certain if it was Wolff's intent, the word, so it seems to me, has come to replace the word "creation" as the preferred scientific and philosophical description of the whole material.[4] The term "cosmology" like the term "creation," understands the world as an "ordered whole" that has integrity in all its parts. But unlike the term "creation," cosmology assumes that this "ordered whole" stands as-a-whole on its own, autonomously, in an absolute sense. Therefore, for cosmology, as both a scientific and philosophical discipline, the question of "origins" is fundamental, and it is assumed that it can be answered in a naturalistic, rational way. To know something's origin is to know it in its totality.

7. Of course, what cosmology dismisses from its outlook is the theological idea of *creatio ex nihilo* (namely, that the world is "created out of nothing") which is, to my knowledge, the only assertion Christian Theology makes about cosmology, the world as whole. Cosmology, in other words, presupposes a "chain of creation," to use Guy Consolmango's term, that can be followed rationally to its beginning, to its origins, which must be some "physical" phenomenon. But Christian Theology says paradoxically that the "source" (meaning, its material origin not its divine maker) of the world-as-a-whole is "nothing." The Creator creates the cosmos *ex nihilo*. This is not a God-of-the-gaps teaching, but one that is rooted, ironically, in Christianity's (and Judaism's) demythologizing, demystifying, indeed, *naturalizing* view of the created world vis-à-vis all spiritualizing tendencies, whether political or religious or philosophical. To say that the creation in all its parts is a "natural" order does not contradict the fact that as-a-whole it exists *ex nihilo*, that is, its existence is absolutely contingent on God the Creator.

8. Moreover, this teaching (*creatio ex nihilo*) is also inseparable from Christianity's understanding of the human person as God's "created co-creator," to use Philip Hefner's pithy term. Humanity is that part of the creation created by God

to be the "steward" (not Lord) of the creation. This, I submit, is the fundamental point of the idea that humanity is created in the image of God. (Gen. 1:26 is theologically consistent with Gen. 2:15). From the perspective of Christian Theology, then, the rise of modern scientific inquiry is a natural, essential aspect of our human vocation as steward, as a species that is accountable how we engage the world. Although Christian Theology holds this self-understanding as an article of faith that can't be proved, yet look how impossible it is to get away from the fact of it. Our very life-together finds us constantly driven to hold each other accountable for our use and abuse of the creation (Cf. Gen. 3:12-13), as though that impulse within us is part of the very warp and woof of the fabric of creation. Yet try to prove it scientifically. You can't.

9. While the idea that God is the Creator who creates *ex nihilo* is an article of faith, it is an article that affirms the scientific sensibility of Occam's razor: Do not add metaphysical entities beyond their need. One danger today is that some Christians want to interpret the Big Bang, for example, as proof of a Creator who creates *ex nihilo* and, thus, the end of cosmology. The irony is that the Christian Doctrine of Creation by definition denies such proof. Therefore, in reality, the Doctrine of Creation says to conscientious scientists, "keep going!" It urges them to look deeper and see farther, if they can, into mystery and wonder of the "natural" astrological-cosmological phenomenon—even that which might lie beyond the Big Bang: not to prove or disprove God, but to further our human vocation to be the stewards and caretakers of this world. There is no hope or danger of either proving or disproving God: such is the nature of the incomprehensible God as the Christian faith asserts. The only danger is false belief: that is, not believing and living as though we are God's stewards and instead believing and living as though we are our own lords. That is the great temptation that is—dare I say—our cosmological "fall" (Genesis 3:4-5), one as Paul asserts has cosmological consequences (Cf. Romans 8:18-25). In the spirit of Augustine, faith by its very nature seeks understanding, but the very thing true faith rests upon—which for him is the Creator God *who is known* to be merciful in Jesus Christ (the soteriological answer to human restlessness)—is finally incomprehensible (cf. *Confession* I.1) to reason and investigation and is accessible only to faith as a divine gift or illumination. But it is believed, not like a fairy tale, but because of the One who spoke it is trustworthy, Jesus Christ, who is not simply the "finger print" of God, but the "finger of God" (Luke 20), the Word made flesh, the soteriological answer to the God problem that every steward faces.

# The Anthropic Principle and Humanity as God's Steward

10. Stephen Barr immerses us into the complex science that underlies the ongoing debate about the meaning and implications of the so-called "Anthropic Principle" (an idea coined by Brandon Carter in 1973) or, as he and others prefer to call it the "anthropic coincidences" (coined earlier by Rob Dicke in 1961). The idea, as I understand it, is linked to our recent knowledge of just how "finely tuned" the cosmic parameters of our universe needed to be microseconds after the Big Bang in order for human life to be as it is in our particular time and place in the universe. For a number of scientists, religionists, and others, this combination of "coincidences" is too fantastic to be simply called "coincidences." Rather, they constitute what is called the Anthropic Principle, the idea that the universe is the logical outworking of some inner purpose or telos, whether mystical or naturalistic, designed to bring forth intelligent human life. We, the human creature, are the ultimate explanation of the cosmos. For many adherents of the Anthropic Principle, the implications of these coincidences for religion is obvious.

11. In my judgment, the Anthropic Principle is a tautology: a statement saying that the world has to be as it is because the world is what it is, a statement that uncritically draws a normative conclusion from a descriptive statement. Moreover, the Anthropic Principle (composed of amazing coincidences) is analogous to the Intelligent Design Theory (rooted in the wonder of irreducible complexity). Neither of these ideas, in my judgment, is science in the modern sense of the term; and neither comes close to anything like proving the existence of God. They may well be expressions of faith in some kind of benevolent Creator-God read into the scientific data, but they are not proof of the Christian God read out of the scientific data. *That* God is by definition incomprehensible, as I explained above. It may also true that the more we scientifically explore the world in which we live the more amazing and awe-inspiring it is—but amazement at the natural world is not proof of a divine Creator.

12. If Christian Theology can speak of something like an "Anthropic Principle" in the world, it would not be deduced from the cosmic constants and it most certainly would not envision humanity as the lord of or the reason for existence of the cosmos. Rather, it would be rooted in something more existential: like our human vocation to be stewards of the creation. The data of this Principle would be twofold, consisting of 1) our innate drive as a species to do science presumably for the sake of a better stewardship of this natural world and 2) our innate sense of holding on another accountable for that stewardship. While those

existential data do not prove the existence of God they do correlate with what Christianity confesses to know about God: 1) that God is the Lord and creator of a cosmos that is wholly other than himself (Gen 1 and 2), 2) that God is the One who has called us into our human role as stewards of the creation (Cf. Gen 1:26-31; 2: 2:15-17), and 3) that God is the one who holds us accountable to him for that stewardship, though it be through the intimate, historical inter-workings of the creation (Genesis 2-3, Rom. 1:18-3:20). Ultimately, the intellectual gifts that God has give humanity are sufficient for us to be stewards, they are not sufficient for us to be lords of creation, that is, to comprehend God or apprehend his deity. But here is also a theological reason also for this intellectual limit: God is generally incomprehensible not only for epistemological reasons, but on account of his wrath, on account of which sinful stewards "suppress the truth" about God (Rom. 1:18). Therefore, any naïve venture into the "existence question" is ultimately fraught with danger and begs a more basic question (basic, that is, to our existence) the "soteriological question: how do stewards survive the wrath of God? The existential data does ultimately corroborate the "soteriological question," rooted in the anxiety-inducing demand that we render an adequate accounting to God for our stewardship (Cf. Luke 16:1-13). Thankfully, the sufficient answer to that question has been historically revealed in no uncertain terms in the Event of Jesus Christ. There is no question about the existence of Jesus Christ, the Word made flesh. The only question is: do we believe him? Do we trust his promise, his claim, to be the One in whom God reconciles to himself the whole cosmos—steward and stars and all? With him, as we believe so we have.

## Endnotes:

1 The brackets contain a summary of an adlib to what I originally wrote in response to the idea of "God's finger prints in the cosmos" that Neyle Sollee had added to his presentation. It is important to add it here because subsequent discussion makes reference to it.

2 For a lucid description of this, see, for example, Philip Cary, "The Incomprehensibility of God and the Origin of the Thomistic Concept of the Supernatural," *Pro Ecclesia* 11, no. 3 (Summer 2002): 340-55.

3 Arvin Vos, Aquinas, *Calvin and Contemporary Protestant Thought: A Critique of Protestant Views of on the thought of Thomas Aquinas* (Grand Rapids, MI: Eerdmans, 1985); Eugene Rogers, Thomas Aquinas and Karl Barth: Sacred Doctrine and the Natural Knowledge of God (Notre Dame, IN: University of Notre Dame Press, 1996); Geisler, Norman L. *Thomas*

*Aquinas: An Evangelical Appraisal.* Grand Rapids: Baker, 1991; Robert L. Reymond, "Dr. John H. Gerstner on Thomas Aquinas as a Protestant," *Westminster Theological Journal* 59.1 (1997): 113-12. For Catholics interested in comparing Aquinas with Protestant thought see, for example, Otto Pesch, The God Question in Thomas Aquinas and Martin Luther (Philadelphia: Fortress Press, 1972); Denis Janz, "Syllogism or Paradox: Aquinas and Luther on Theological Method," *Theological Studies*, vol. 59, 1998, pages 3-21.

4 Tore Frangsmyr, "Christian Wolff's Mathematical Method and its Impact on the Eighteenth Century," *Journal of the History of Ideas*, Vol. 36, No. 4 (Oct. - Dec., 1975), pp. 653-668.

# Contemplating the Divine: a Response to the Essayists

**Sebastian Mahfood**
**Kenrick-Glennon Seminary**

Sebastian Mahfood, PhD is Associate Professor of Intercultural Studies at Kenrick-Glennon Seminary in St. Louis, Missouri. He holds from St Louis University a doctoral degree in postcolonial literature, a subject in which he developed an interest while teaching at the University of Kairouan in Tunisia, North Africa, during his two-year service to the United States Peace Corps. Mahfood also serves as coordinator of instructional technology and coordinator of the Global Vision Initiative. He lives in St. Louis with his wife, Dr. Stephanie Mahfood, and son, Alexander. At present, he is completing coursework on a distance learning masters of arts in philosophy through Holy Apostles College and Seminary in Cromwell, Connecticut, and working on a book about the use of appropriate technologies in theological teaching and learning. Recently, he accepted an invitation to became a member of the ITEST Board with the unanimous approval of the Board of Directors.

Welcome to a short talk entitled "Contemplation on the Divine" prepared in response to the presentations delivered at the 2007 symposium on Cosmology and Astronomy sponsored by the Institute for the Theological Encounter with Science and Technology. My name is Dr. Sebastian Mahfood, Associate Professor of Intercultural Studies, at Kenrick-Glennon Seminary in St. Louis, MO.

To skip through a brief history of scientific thought, we can start with where we began recording, with Plato's dialogue "The Meno," in which Socrates explains that knowing is a form of remembering our pre-incarnate existence in which all truth was held in universal forms. Aristotle, Plato's greatest student, reformed this view by introducing the concept of the syllogism, where two things known give birth to a third thing previously unknown. Using this formula, Aristotle brought us to the height and the light of human reason. Stephen Barr has shared with us the idea "[t]hat the universe is life-bearing is not something that we can take for granted; rather, it should be seen as a very remarkable fact, a fact that can be seen, even without faith, as pointing to God." And that was Aristotle's aim, which we know from his *Metaphysics*, that all of philosophy was an exercise in understanding who we are in relation to our source. With the advent of Christianity, the epistemological system changed. Divine Revelation was made available, and it didn't destroy the role played by reason; rather, it helped us understand it better through the Apostle Paul's articulation of theory of natural law in Romans 2:15, the law written by God on men's hearts, which the Catechism (paragraph 1955) defines as "nothing other than the light of understanding placed in us by God [through which we know] what we must do and what we must avoid." We now had two systems that could work together, but there was a gulf, as Br. Guy demonstrated yesterday quoting St. Augustine's polemic against the early Christians who spoke against the prevailing cosmology, between Aristotle, or natural reality, on the one hand and Sacred Scripture, or supernatural reality, on the other.

It was St. Thomas, in his scholastic enterprise, who definitively brought the two worlds together, accomplishing what Joseph Pieper calls the bending of Odysseus's bow, which, if you'll remember from your mythology, was a task only the superhuman Odysseus could do upon his return from the war and his travels. Following this height of the synthesis of human reason and divine revelation came a series of reductions. I'll just list the big three, each of whom, according to Jacques Maritain's *Integral Humanism,* initiated a new wave of man's fragmentation from God. The first began with Niccolò Machiavelli (early-16th century), who fragmented man's relationship with himself through his focus on power and political organizations that maintained its balance. The second began with

Jean-Jacques Rousseau (mid-18th century), who fragmented man's relationship with nature with his ideas of the evolution of human sapience (something Charles Darwin would later bring to its completion with his evolution of the human body) and man's natural holiness. The third began with Friedrich Nietzsche (late-19th century), who fragmented man's relationship with the divine through his deification of man.

Let's take another look at the scheme of Dante's Inferno that Br. Guy showed us – remember, at the time, hell was a real place right beneath the terrestrial plane. We literally walked on top of it. Dante, who drew a great deal of his insight in the development of his cosmos from St. Thomas, divides hell into three phases – separation of man from man (circles 1-7 to the second round), separation of man from nature (circle 7, round 3, and most of circle 8), and separation of man from God (overlapping circle 8 and circle 9). See a pattern? Dante knew that once we began on the path of separating ourselves from love of man, who is prior in knowledge, we'd ultimately separate ourselves from love of God, who is prior in being. At the very bottom of his hell is a lake of ice, the center of which contains Lucifer, surrounded by souls so trapped within it that they've lost the power of movement and become inert beings incapable of communion with anyone. Now, this isn't meant to be reductive. The scientific revolution that began in the Renaissance continues to teach us a great deal about ourselves and our place in the universe. It's merely meant to demonstrate that we've been moving away from the synthesis St. Thomas demonstrates between natural and divine law. Our Catholic epistemology, our synthesis between reason and faith of how we know what it is we know, has been steadily compromised for the past seven hundred years, culminating in what we now call the problem of post-modernity, which reached its height in the 1992 Supreme Court decision of Planned Parenthood v. Casey, in which the court established that "At the heart of liberty is the right to define one's own concept of existence, of meaning, of the universe, and of the mystery of human life." Here, we've finally hit bottom.

At least when we hit the bottom, we know enough to pick ourselves up. We start to realize that maybe there are things out there that we really don't know, and we come, like Socrates, who for all his epistemological foibles, began with the search for wisdom as his foundation rather than ever believing he had attained it. What it takes, as Br. Guy notes, is a turn of perspective, is a looking at something from another angle to realize that there are dimensions to our existence that are beyond our knowing. If we look upon these dimensions as *metaphorical* multiverses, then we've acknowledged at least a need to step back from ourselves and explore the mystery of the Other, and that's what makes the idea of a multiverse attractive, that we have another bow of Odysseus that, Stephen explains, could be strung through an exploration of what it means that our living in a multiverse may be seen as an anthropic coincidence, that the conditions of our world have set in motion a process that is presently being articulated in the set of conditions necessary for us to have come together in this room – I'm speaking, of course, of thousands of years of preparation on the part not of us but of our ancestors. Within this teleologically-oriented multiverse in which we exist, we have a perspective that we should try to understand with the help of Divine wisdom, with the help of Christ who fully reveals mankind to himself. To do that, we have to contextualize our consciousness within reality. Now, this is where it gets fun. According to string theory, for instance, as articulated by Rob Bryanton in his book, *Imagining the Tenth Dimension,* in 2-D land, there is no concept of a 3 dimensional object. Flatlanders would perceive a balloon moving through their world, for instance, in the form of a pinpoint that expands and hollows as large as its diameter will allow, then shrinks back to the size of a pinpoint. Conversely, those beings that live outside of time would experience, like Billy Pilgrim's captors in *Slaughterhouse Five,* the human person in our four-dimensional world as long cords with one end resting inside of another and the other, at some indeterminate point, resting inside the earth, and, as far as our eternal destinies are concerned, branching beyond it like a caterpillar that turns into a butterfly leaving his cocoon behind.

Our realization of new dimensions to our existence may generate transformations in consciousness, but it doesn't in any way affect who we are as human persons. As St. Thomas teaches us, divine revelation did not destroy reason but fulfilled it. Like the fish who learns more about the world it's in by encountering a snow globe, we can agree with Br. Guy that "[t]he most important aspects of these challenges are not in the confrontation of new facts to old theories, religious or scientific" but "in how they reveal the unrecognized assumptions we have made in our previous understanding of heaven and earth, and by extension the assumptions we have made in our understanding of God as the creator of earth and heaven." Our encountering new understandings of how existence works should, therefore, confirm our faith in a subsistent being who is, as St. Thomas describes, pure act and pure essence. Einstein's desire to know the mind of God, though an impossible thing to achieve, should be matched by our own, and this is the purpose of Catholic metaphysics as a contemplative science. What we can do, though, is much simpler, and that's to take, as Neyle articulates, "the opportunity to make a free, non-coercive choice to open ourselves to the transforming power of God," to open ourselves to a mystery that no Supreme Court decision can legislate.

For this, we need to allow our growing understanding to continue to glorify God, for St. Thomas wrote in Question 5, Answer 5, of his *Summa Theologica* – "The ultimate happiness prepared for the saints exceeds man's intellect and will, for the Apostle says in 1 Cor. 2.9, 'Eye hath not seen, nor ear heard, neither *hath it entered into the heart of man*, what things God hath prepared for them that love him.' Therefore, man cannot achieve happiness by his natural powers." He can achieve it only through his participation with the Divine, and participation has two forms – the 1st is liturgical, which is man's participation in the activity of God, and the second is grace, which is God's participation in the activity of man. We come to know the world through our senses as Aristotle teaches in the *Metaphysics*, and we have a natural understanding of the world written on our hearts, as the Apostle Paul writes in Romans, but we come to God only through supernatural faith, which is an active response to divine revelation. In this light, it does matter the good that we pursue, for there are many goods to which we are attracted – if we didn't perceive at least a particular good within them, then we wouldn't be attracted to them – but there is only one good that is *necessary*, as Christ explains to Martha in Luke 10: 28-32, and that is being in the presence of and contemplating the Divine.

So, that brings us to the point. It may be a fine thing for a secular society that has lost its sense of mystery to consider the meaning of human liberty to reside in the arbitration of one's own destiny – we all have that liberty predicated by our free will - but it is a poverty for persons created in the image and likeness of God to willfully and intellectually divorce ourselves as creatures from the Creator. It's to choose the dark side of manipulation and exploitation of man when there can only be one saving choice. In stopping the violence of our ripping ourselves away from our Creator, Maritain argues in *Integral Humanism* that we need to regain our humanism by working towards a functional reintegration of ourselves with others within the human community and with God. We may have learned a lot in our short residency on this planet, and the greatest evidence of that lies in our understanding that we know very little in comparison with the Divine intellect that can contemplate so much substance and thought that lie beyond our philosophies, but there really only is one thing necessary, and all our science should turn us in that direction, whatever, wherever, and whenever, as Br. Guy has explained, that may be.

Now this, of course, brings with it a challenge – an evangelical vocation – if we do find sapient life out there in worlds presently beyond our comprehension. We don't yet know how we'll reach them, but we do know one thing for sure. Christ came here to planet Earth. To address Thomas Paine's ridiculing the idea of a savior who had to die over and over again, we have the model of Christ's sacrifice in a particular place and time. He didn't die in Europe, in Asia, in Africa, in S. or N. America, or in Australia, but his message reaches these places. He didn't die in Barnard's star system, but we spiritual descendants of the Apostolic tradition will evangelize those worlds, too. Just as John Paul II brought the Church into cyberspace so that people there would find the Church, we, too, will evangelize the multiverse. We can't not, and our epistemological grounding will come when a new St. Thomas – every major breakthrough in human thought needs its own St. Thomas, and who knows but that Stephen Barr might be ours – when a new St. Thomas arises from among us, someone who will be able to do for the new science what St. Thomas did for Aristotle.

*l to r: F. Muller, Fr. E. Muller, V. White*

*l to r: John Cross, S. Kuhl*

# Astronomy/Cosmology Breakthroughs and the God Question

## Session 2

*Proceedings of the ITEST Symposium - September, 2007*

**Greenley:**    This question relates to what was brought up in the last session: that of time. For instance, what did God do before He created time and the universe? How do we even talk about the concept of time in relation to God and creation?

**Sheahen:**    I'd be happy to respond to that question myself since I feel like an authority having written so many essays on it; St. Augustine was as clear as a bell on this. That question is not a meaningful question because God was the creator of all space and time, and *that* was the beginning of creation. Under those circumstances there is no such thing as the word "before." You can't ask a question about "before" God created time.

**Greenley:**    But that's the question everyone seems to be asking in the community.

**Sheahen:**    That's a mistake on the part of human beings and it reflects a limitation that humans bring to the table; but we must never confuse that with a limitation upon God. That's the crucial point…

**Greenley:**    …that God is infinite…

**Sheahen**:    It is a human limitation to think that everything has to happen in time because *we* are conditioned that way… but God is not.

**Barr:**    I want to react to the reaction to our presentations provided by Steven Kuhl, the responder. I agree with much of what you said, Steve, but I have to take issue with your emphasis on a few of the things you brought up.

You deal with the question of the existence of God. I understood you to say (and perhaps I understood wrongly) that that was not really a major concern of the biblical authors. For example in the first chapter of Romans some scholars use this as an example of a passage dealing with the question of the existence of God. You seem to be saying that the real concern of that passage is something very different. I'm not so sure that's true.

My understanding, and the Scripture scholars present may correct me, is that the entire background of the first chapter of Romans is based on or draws from the material in the 13th chapter of Wisdom. Whether or not that is true, the 13th chapter of the book of Wisdom was clearly concerned with the question of the existence of God. In fact, of all the passages in the Bible that one, I think, is the most relevant to the whole body of science and religion passages. It was written in the first Century BC and it was in a sense addressed to Ancient Greece, to Greek wisdom and philosophy. It was in a sense addressed to the scientists of those days. It does ask the question: How is it that these learned and wise people understand so much about the physical world and how it operates, and see so much of the power and beauty of the things of this natural world? And yet they fail to recognize that the source of all that beauty and power is the Creator.

The Book of Wisdom *does* talk about the existence of God and how He can be recognized in the beauty and power of the natural world So I think it *is* a concern. It also was the concern of some of the early Christian apologists. One of my favorite passages is from a Latin Christian Apologist Minucius Felix who lived around 200 AD. He wrote: "If upon entering some home you saw that everything was well-tended, neat and decorative, you would believe that some master was in charge of it and that he was himself much superior to those good things. So too, in the home of this world when you see providence, order and law in the heavens and on Earth, believe that there is a Lord and Author of the universe more beautiful than the stars themselves and the various parts of the whole world."

Now that is an argument for the existence of God from the order and law in nature. Again the question of the existence of God and its recognizability from the natural world is certainly a concern of the early Christian writers, not just from philosophers and others. It's a concern of St Augustine, Thomas Aquinas. So I reject the idea that this question is not Biblical . However I agree with you – it's not the *only* question and it's not the most important question. The existence of a designer or fashioner of the natural world and its laws, may not be the most important question to most people. There are more existential questions: Who am I? What is my destiny? How ought I to live? How can I achieve happiness, fulfillment? How can I be saved? Those are more important questions, I agree.

But I think the question of the existence of God, and the attempt to see God in the natural world or see him through the natural world, is an important question.

I have another criticism. In your response to the papers you used the phrase "...the questions that theology is interested in addressing." You seemed to say, that the question of the existence of God is not one of the "questions theology is interested in addressing." Well, I think that theologians should be interested in addressing not only "the questions that theology is interested in addressing," but all the questions of ordinary people, who are not theologians.

I've read some books on science and religion written by theologians: Catholic and Protestant. But those theologians are addressing other theologians. In other words they are addressing those who already believe in God and their concern is: how we can incorporate the findings of science into revising our theology? I think a more important audience may be people who don't believe in God: many in the scientific community, many people who are not scientists but may be influenced by scientific modes of thought, who don't believe in God in the first place. Their questions may be the ones some theologians are not interested in addressing.

But these people are interested in the question. "Why should I believe in God in the first place?" "Why does the whole idea of God make sense in the life of a scientist?" So, the question of the existence of God is very important to a lot of people.

I want to add another point: A mistake made by scientists and theologians alike is that they ask more of science than it can give. Sometimes we get disappointed in science because it can't give us answers. The three of us here, the presenters, are scientists. We can tell you something about the orderliness of the universe, anthropic coincidences, and so on. We can tell you about Minucius Felix's providence, order and law in the heavens and on Earth. But we can't tell you about soteriology, not as scientists; nor about the Incarnation of Christ — as scientists; nor about the Gospel message. So of course, the kinds of things scientists can contribute within the religion/science dialogue are going to seem threadbare and perhaps a little pallid compared to the full depth and richness of the Christian Faith. But that's the way it is. Don't ask from science and scientists more than they can give.

**Kuhl:** First of all I was talking about the "proof" of the existence of God. That God exists is a pre-supposition of scriptures, I think, for the most part, and for Christian theology. So, "First Principles," if you will, is not theology's focus – you asked me to look at Wisdom 13 in regard to that.

**Barr:** Especially verses 1- 9

**Kuhl:** There is a kind of irony in your asking me that question because this book is in the Roman Catholic canon and not in the canon for all Protestants. My point is that the Lutheran tradition follows Jerome on this and the Roman Catholic tradition, in terms of the canon, follows Augustine. And, of course, the creation of an "official" list of the Old Testament canon didn't happen until after the 16th century Reformation when the Council of Trent decided what constituted its Old Testament. There are a variety of reasons why everyone chose what they chose, but it's a very complicated question.

Nevertheless, I do have a version of the Bible that includes Wisdom as part of the Apocryphal writings and I'm looking at verse 5 ….

**Barr:**   Why don't you just read verses 1 – 9? It's addressed to scientists.

**Kuhl:**

1For all people who were ignorant of God were foolish by nature; and they were unable from the good things that are seen to know the one who exists, nor did they recognize the artisan while paying heed to his works;

2but they supposed that either fire or wind or swift air, or the circle of the stars, or turbulent water, or the luminaries of heaven were the gods that rule the world.

3If through delight in the beauty of these things people assumed them to be gods, let them know how much better than these is their Lord, for the author of beauty created them.

4And if people were amazed at their power and working, let them perceive from them how much more powerful is the one who formed them.

5For from the greatness and beauty of created things comes a corresponding perception of their Creator.

6Yet these people are little to be blamed, for perhaps they go astray while seeking God and desiring to find him.

7For while they live among his works, they keep searching, and they trust in what they see, because the things that are seen are beautiful.

8Yet again, not even they are to be excused;

9for if they had the power to know so much that they could investigate the world, how did they fail to find sooner the Lord of these things?

*- New Revised Standard Version*

It *is* a beautiful passage, but I'm not sure it's a passage that is saying that one could prove the existence of God by looking at the creation of the world. On the contrary, it's talking about the difficulty of doing that; it's talking about the beauty of the world; and that beauty is idolatrously equated by people with divinity. But I want to be clear. I am not saying that the existence of God isn't an important question. I'm saying that it cannot be proved from a rationalist, scientific point of view… from perception and the investigation of the world.

But as I read this passage in Wisdom, as people are described there, a key passage is verse three: "If through delight in the beauty of these things, people assume them to be gods, let them know how much better than these is their Lord." And that's a key point: we get so interested in creation, and so awe-inspired by creation that we tend to deify it. That seems to be the natural impulse of so many people, as Wisdom diagnoses them. And so, how do you overcome that natural impulse that seems to be there? People like us, he says, we are "…to let them know how much better than these is their Lord, for the author of beauty created them."

There is an inherent evangelistic element, and component, that is an essential part of the way this God is made known and that is at the heart and core of the Wisdom literature itself. It's not about using our scientific means and methods of investigation. For the writer of Wisdom, God is not discovered, rather God reveals God's self. You're not going to find God by searching the creation, although it is certainly true that it is God who has created it. For the believer that statement is obvious; for the non-believer, for whatever reason, it is not very obvious. But in Wisdom, it is not the atheist conclusion that is being confronted; but the deification of the created world that is being confronted.

Now let's look at some other passages about these believers in this very book of Wisdom. Let's see how "Augustinian," if you will, this writer is. Chapter 4 describes some people who perceive God and with whom God is pleased (verse 10). They perceived God, not because they were so scientifically intelligent, but because they were elect, they perceived because they received grace and mercy (verse 15). It is a soteriological statement. The others, called the peoples, did not so understand nor did they pay attention to them — and their testimony. And why is that so? Here the Wisdom writer says, "Yet the peoples saw and did not understand, or take such a thing to heart, that God's grace and mercy are with his elect and that he watches over his holy ones" (verse 15).

Here is the great mystery. What is the stance he asks of us who believe in this God whom we have come to know by being the elect? How do we come to know God? The stance in the world we are to take then, is like this: from Chapters 4 and 5

> 4:20They will come with dread when their sins are reckoned up, and their lawless deeds will convict them to their face.

> 5:1Then the righteous will stand with great confidence in the presence of those who have oppressed them and those who make light of their labours.

> 2When the unrighteous see them, they will be shaken with dreadful fear, and they will be amazed at the unexpected salvation of the righteous.
> *- New Revised Standard Version*

But, this is what will happen: "They will speak to one another in repentance and in anguish of spirit they will groan and say, 'these are the persons we once held in derision, and made a byword of reproach' — fools that we are!" (verse 3). In other words there is a profoundly deep personal evangelistic witness that somehow accompanies the knowledge, understanding and reality of God. It has a profound mystical and mysterious element, which is very much like what Augustine talks about in his *Confessions*. In the *Confessions*, Augustine says it's not by reason that I found God; God found me. When Augustine used reason, he found the Manichees; and he thought that they were the source of the most reasonable religion there could be, melding together the material world and the spiritual world. But concerning that world says Augustine, it is foolishness. And of course neo-Platonism forged a language to talk about this mystical kind of "being captured by God." But it is not about proof in any scientific sense.

But I'm not saying that the question of the existence of God isn't important. My question is: "how does the existence of God become known to the world?" I think, at least in the passage you asked me to look at, Dr. Barr, there is a profound evangelical aspect to it. I hope that makes sense. At least that's how I read it.

Finally, I do see myself as an Apologist. I see the Wisdom literature as an *apologia*. But the place where apologetics emerges for these people, I think, is at the level of the existential.

**Barr:**   You raised an interesting point that I meant to mention before. I think the question of proof is a red herring. I agree with what Br. Guy said earlier. Science is not a matter of proofs in a sense of deductive proofs, of rigorous demonstration. That's not what science is about; it never has been about that. In mathematics one makes rigorous deductive proofs. One doesn't do that in empirical science. One has an explanation, a theory which makes sense of some set of data in the sensible world. And to the extent that some theory or some set of assumptions allows one to explain a large number of things, to make sense of a large number of things, then you become convinced that your explanation is correct or at least you are on the right track.

So, again, the question of "proofs" is a red herring. The question remains: can we find evidence in the world around us that there is a creator? Are there grounds for belief? Grounds, not proofs. But if a rational foundation or ground of our belief in God rests to some extent on the nature of the world in which we live. I think the answer is "Yes."

Here, I emphasize, and I'm sure you know this, that for a Catholic, one of the important statements from the first Vatican Council (1869-1870) was contained in the chapter dealing with Faith and Reason.[1] One of the concerns of the first Vatican Council was the whole question of science and modern rationalism and so on. Vatican I makes very clear that our faith — though faith is a gift from God — is not based solely on deductions or proofs; it is also rational. It stresses that there *are* rational grounds for belief. Furthermore, if there were no rational grounds for belief, then our belief would be contrary to reason.

Remember, it emphasizes very strongly that our belief *is* rational. It is what St Paul calls a "reasonable service."

So, of course, our faith is not based on "proofs;" our faith is rational. It is based to some extent on "evidence." It's important though, in talking with atheists, not to quote scripture to them. Yes, scripture presupposes that God exists, of course. The people of Israel, the people of the New Testament, the Jewish audiences whom Jesus addressed, presuppose that God exists. But the people we talk to today do not have that presupposition. Therefore we must be able and willing to show them that belief in God has a rational foundation

**Muller, Francisco:**   I have another question, but let me first comment on what

---

1 See Session 3 of the First Vatican Council: Dogmatic Constitution on the Catholic Faith, Chapter 4 "On faith and reason."

you were saying. You were talking about Vatican I. Most people don't know that Vatican I condemned Fideism, that is, condemned "pure faith" without reason. On the other hand it also condemned the opposite error, "Ontologism" which is reason alone, without faith. Vatican I prescribed both things for us: faith and reason, exactly the same thing done by John Paul II in his encyclical "Fides et Ratio." Remember his beautiful comparison at the beginning of that letter: *"Faith and reason are like the two wings on which the human spirit rises to the contemplation of truth."* Thus, we need the two wings. This is our precious Catholic tradition; we unite reason and faith, being neither "fideists" nor "rationalists." When the Pope mentioned the word "truth" as a goal of "reason" he is putting us into the realm of "philosophy," which is nothing but the "love of truth." And philosophy is like a middle terrain between Science on the one hand and Theology on the other. Unfortunately in all these debates about science and faith we go too quickly from theology to science and vice versa. We don't stop long enough in that middle rational terrain which is purely human. Dwelling in it is the reason why philosophers like Socrates, Plato and Aristotle could discover God. Yes, not the God of Christianity, but God anyway, a real achievement of their human intelligence.

Using, therefore, philosophical methods and arguments, we can (and we must) say that God can be proven. With rational arguments, not *a priori* (as wrongly pretended by St. Anselm), but *a posteriori*, after the facts of the existing things, we can know God. There are many ways of doing this, as in the famous "Five Ways" of Aquinas. But the most complete and deep one is by the whole study of metaphysics which could be described as a rational inquiry and journey which starts with finite (multiple and changing) beings, to conclude on the necessity of an Infinite Being, which exists "by itself" and founds the whole of reality.

In short, the word "proof" is not a heretical word for the Christian. Only that we have to understand it not in a scientific way (where "proof" is never final) nor on a mathematical way (where "proof" refers to mere logical and numerical abstractions).

Now to my question about the anthropic principle, which is one of the first topics mentioned by Stephen Barr. Can the anthropic principle be considered, or "used" also as a "heuristic principle," helping scientists to discover new things? For example, somebody like Fred Hoyle, certainly not suspected of philosophy much less of religiosity, asked himself why Carbon is so abundant? Suspecting that the reason was "because it is needed for life," he investigated the rate of nucleosynthesis going on in the stars, only to discover an exquisite resonance phenomena[2] in favor of the fusion of Carbon nuclei, so finely tuned, that it explains the abundance we see today. The funny thing is that physicists never discovered this before Hoyle, simply because they were not looking for it. So it seems that the anthropic principle was a realistic guide in this case, wasn't it?

**Barr:** There is certainly another instance where someone tried to explain something in physics by means of anthropic argument. I wrote in my paper that for decades people were trying to understand why something called the cosmological constant was zero. Theorists generally took it for granted that this parameter was exactly zero. But still nobody understands why, and that is one of the great unsolved problems in physics. Steve Weinberg suggested that perhaps the explanation of why this cosmological constant was close to zero was — he tried to explain it with an anthropic argument – that only if the cosmological constant is very small could we be here. But the anthropic argument doesn't tell you that it's zero; it just tells you that it's less than a certain magnitude which is quite close to what the experimental limits were at that time. Lo and behold, after about 11 years or so, assuming that the dark energy is the cosmological constant, it seems that there is a cosmological constant, and it's not zero. Weinberg's explanation would lead you to expect that it *would* be there and it would not be zero. But in a sense, he almost predicted what was found 11 years later. That's the closest I can come to an example leading to something like a prediction.

**Sheahen:** In his book *Insight* of 1956, Lonergan points out the idea of being in a heuristic situation in which you are motivated to think and look for discoveries because of the profound scientific questions before your eyes. *Insight* treats the question of how we understand things. Lonergan goes on in that part of the book to explain how that thinking process proceeds.

**McNamara:** A comment on your use of the language! William Dembski, one of the founders of Intelligent Design argument, uses the term epistemic support. What he finds in science is this epistemic support for his belief. So that's one term that could be used here. But I have another question; it's been floating around here through this whole discussion. It's a question of time. You've already seen from your "coincidences," as it were, that any shorter time but yet at least sufficient for the ten million life span of the G-star or sun, we wouldn't be here. And if it were too short then we go back to the four forces of nature that have to be at a certain magnitude in order for that to happen. Without that the

2 It was Fred Hoyle who first noticed the three-helium resonance that produces carbon inside of stars. Without that, no heavier elements would have been formed, hence no planets, no people, and so on. It's an important "anthropic" coincidence or principle. (eds.)

star's lifetime wouldn't be long enough; we wouldn't have the planet formed or it would be too long and die out.

Are we being told from the theological viewpoint, therefore, that time is what it is – and this would be another anthropological coincidence, because God wants to reveal himself through time. He wants people to develop slowly and go through these different stages. Maybe even because he knows that it is going to take that much time for people to actually understand the God who does not manifest himself in all kinds of glory and power. That is a whole misunderstanding of the servant.

Christ said, I am not going to be the glorious Messiah; I am not going to be a David Messiah, not a political Messiah. I am going to be a suffering Messiah. That's so counter to the ordinary human expectations: that God would purposely choose that role. Therefore, we need that much time in order to understand what God *is* – not our image of Him which would make him glorious, but the God who is in Jesus Christ. I'm proposing that time has to be discussed here also.

**Muller, Earl:** What caught my attention, of course, was the presupposition of the Old Testament and the existence of God. I teach Fundamental Theology and there have been two different understandings of how fundamental theology works. The more classical, Thomism understands fundamental theology as dealing with "first things:" the things that we have to consider or put into place prior to the act of faith which brings us into scripture which in turn leads us into the realm of theology proper. The way that fundamental theology is supposed to operate under that mode is through reason alone. We work with proofs for the existence of God, proofs for the immortality of the soul, demonstrations that revelation is possible and then finally get to the point where we look at the world to see if there is evidence for claiming that revelation has indeed taken place.

Lonergan, in his work *Method in Theology*, shifted the focus of fundamental theology to a different approach where what we are looking at is the structure of the faith of the believer. Here we get into a different kind of presupposition. Soteriology, as Christians understand it, presupposes the passion death and resurrection of Christ. Believing that that Paschal Mystery has power to save, presupposes that Christ is God; presupposing that Christ is God, presupposes that there is a God. Even for the faith of the believer, there is this structure. As one goes down deeper, one eventually reaches the level of belief in God.

So there are two different models for explaining how the concept of the existence of God functions within theology. The first one is the only one that really presumes that we are working here with pure reason. Proofs for the existence of God, apart from demonstrations of the rationality of the proofs strictly speaking, or the beauty of the creation, or anthropic coincidences, create wonder within us. They strike us as special, as perhaps connoting something more than appears simply on the surface.

There is a presupposition in moving from that experience of wonder to the conclusion that there is a God. One of the presuppositions is that of a realist philosophy, that there is something out there corresponding with what's going on in my mind. We speak of this in terms of knowledge in general. But in terms of proofs for God's existence, it particularly works in moving from what our mind is doing to the affirmation that there is something in reality that corresponds to it.

Traditional metaphysical proofs for Gods existence can be understood as instances of Gödel's theorem. The first three of the Thomistic proofs are based on an analysis of Aristotelian act-potency structure. Aristotle's presupposition is that both the universe and things in the universe are intrinsically intelligible. The problem is that, as a logical system, potency analysis cannot support itself. That analysis at its root can be supported only from outside the system. So what Aristotle and Thomas have to do is to move from act-potency analysis to the affirmation of pure act which breaks the Aristotelian correlation of the system. From Gödel we can see the necessity of making a move of that sort. The question is: does the structure of our mind correspond to reality? There is a presupposition here. The believer is willing to say "Yes, It does correspond to something out there." The atheist entertains the possibility that we are simply delusional and that what's going on in our mind has no necessary correlation with reality outside the mind.

This was one of the important things John Paul II pointed out in his encyclical, *Fides et Ratio*. The philosophy that will serve as a way of unpacking the faith has to be a realist philosophy. We have to be convinced that our mind can know reality and that the structures of logic in our minds correspond to reality, that the sense of wonder we experience — for instance, the Big Bang, the Beauty of creation, or anthropic coincidences — corresponds to something. If we accept that presupposition then we can talk about proofs, but it's not going to be a proof to anyone unwilling to make that presupposition about the relationship of the human mind to reality.

**Sheahen:**   I want to add something to that about what we can prove and what we can't prove. For all the discussion that lasted for centuries and centuries about proving the existence of God and so on, Gödel came along in the 1930s and undercut a great deal of that thinking by showing that there are really statements that are true; you know that they are true, but you cannot prove them. An excellent exposition of this whole thing and why it's so important for an understanding of what we can and cannot prove, is in Stephen Barr's book, *Modern Physics and Ancient Faith*, 211- 220, where he discusses that very question.

**McGuire:**   I want to touch on several different things from several different people. I have more of an observation rather than a question from my area of theology rather than of science. Neyle Sollee made a statement "that science becomes religion's handmaid when it opens us to wonder, awe, beauty and a sense of mystery, and then again addressing the mystery of God."

My sense out of all these conversations is prompted by something Stephen Barr said about the question not being about the existence of God but evidence of God, and I add "which we call revelation." Christians understand God as revealed. So we ask how, where and when do I encounter God? How to I get to know God more or better? Where is my "scientia" of God? There have been a lot of inferences about nature and grace, faith and reason and in the last century and a half we have moved sometimes very radically from the scholastic philosophical understanding of nature versus grace and faith versus reason to bridging the two. I think Karl Rahner, for one, made a brilliant contribution to the question of grace where he moved beyond that dialectic. In effect grace is not something *alongsid*e nature but it is *through* nature that we are *engraced.*

Do we have the evidence of the existence of God or how do we know when God reveals himself to us? Rahner would say God is constantly being revealed to us; we are just not always aware of this.

If we understand God as revealed, we also, as Christians, understand God as Trinitarian, as inherently relational which is a dynamic principle. I use "dynamic" because for me that says so much about what science has contributed to our knowledge of the universe, of everything. There's a dynamism about it. So the relationality that we use theologically about the Trinity, the Godhead, to me bridges over to science and to some of the concepts that science brings to this weekend. My dynamic principle at heart – understanding and knowing God — fits really well into the multiverse understanding of the cosmos. It's difficult to know if the universe is the smaller or the larger domain (cosmos, universe). It isn't just a question of order; rather, it is one of a relationality between "orders," if you will, and for me that's just another stamp of God's revelation.

**Cross:** I'd like to take a little time to talk about time. This is what my wife would call "nut talk." As a cognitive psychologist, I'm very interested in the concept of time and the evolution of consciousness. It seems to me that Immanuel Kant made great contributions to understanding human consciousness. The notion of consciousness leads us to think in terms of time, space and causality — human structures, if you will. The thing is that once you become conscious of these limiting categories of thought, you try to circumvent them. Theology becomes the exploration of the eternal, spatially unlimited realms of Being: trying to see things as God sees them. In cosmology and theology we speculate about a multiverse without beginning or end, in which every event has some effect in every place beyond the origin of the event. The developing unity in Christian theology! I think that's the nature of the evolution of consciousness. We become more and more conscious of consciousness. When we do that, we recognize that our human consciousness is unlike that of animals who are not aware of their consciousness. We are critical about our consciousness. The evolution of consciousness has brought about this growing criticism. So the evolution of scientific method is also evidence of that kind of careful awareness of limitations of our own awareness of things.

With respect to the question of time, when we look at the history of science, it is the history of an increasing capacity to look for instance, at the very long and very short events that occur in the cloud chamber or the accelerator, or the events that take place in the origin and strata of geology in the Grand Canyon or better; the Big Bang.

Animals have no ability to delve into this dimension of time, and the dimension of space is the same, for instance with the microscope, the telescope and so on. The infinitesimal strings of super symmetry theory and the reality which may exist beyond the speed of light-horizon of the known universe, are examples. This history of science is a history of expanding our consciousness of space and time.

For me, Teilhard de Chardin provides a good example of the whole history of philosophy and of theology. His notion of evolving complexity, the uniquely organized complexity which makes both our brain and our consciousness possible, represents a motion from matter. What is matter? Matter is that which is limited to space and time. But we investigate space and time. The more we do so, the more we move away from the usual identification of what is material to that which is spiritual, which in turn moves toward a *space time infinity* continuum rather than the exaggerated matter-spirit dualism of Cartesian thinking. From a psychologist's viewpoint this is a way of looking at relativity theory — the cognitive relativity of space and time and causality.

**Streeter:**   I'd like to piggy-back on John Cross' observations and that is, the question with faith and reason or nature and grace is always – "where do they occur?" That's my question. They don't hang on some bungee cord from some cloud. They go on within consciousness. So they are always mediated somehow by consciousness, by our humanness, by our human consciousness. So it really behooves us to pay attention to what's going on there. And I allude to a very simple metaphor in contradistinction to the "layered look" of nature and grace: nature is the base and then a layer of grace goes on and somehow elevates nature. That is the older view of the nature/grace dynamic.

More too, let's go back to the sacramental ritual (for those of us who are Catholic here). In our sacramental ritual we use oil constantly as a sacramental sign of anointing. Try this simple experiment. Put some olive oil in a little saucer, dip Kleenex into that olive oil, then have your children sit with you and watch it. You will watch with amazement, of course, that the oil climbs the Kleenex. The Kleenex does not disappear, but it will never be the same again. You can distinguish the oil and the Kleenex, but you cannot separate them. That is a more appropriate view of the nature/grace dynamic.

That's how grace builds on nature – the interpenetration of the Divine with the consciousness of that individual, of that person and of the church. The spirit is very often portrayed by oil, fire, water, wind and wine. These images point to the fact that the Spirit "lubricates" our often hesitant human decisions; the Spirit cauterizes in us what needs to be burned away; it cleanses; it "blows out' the staleness in us; it makes us intoxicated at times with joy in life. In these dynamic sacramental images we are learning much about how that which is mystery is going to interpenetrate our consciousness. We will know that because we will behave differently.

There is a theological position that there is no such thing as pure nature. I'm not talking about purity here, I'm talking about nature acting alone, where we not only distinguish the oil from the Kleenex, but say they can be separated. The theological understanding would be that nature can *never* be without the influence of that creative power of God. Never! It can't function. That's what contingency means. That's what it means to have the human come forth from the divine – that creative-wise you can't even draw a breath without the power of God. That's one thing: the grace dynamic characterized by reciprocal friendship, relationality between the human subject and God. This never does away with nature's distinct functioning.

Those things need to be distinguished, but then we move to the paradigm of the nature and grace interpenetration. Then we might begin to understand too what the Incarnation is trying to teach us about the permeation of the Word with our humanness so that we have this hypostatic union in Christ in that humanness. Where is the divinity of Jesus? Where is it? In the consciousness of his humanness, of instrumental sacred humanity.

Athanasius says that they are not mixed up like a beaten egg. They are totally distinct and yet they are interpenetrated. What is that telling us about us? About nature/grace? What is it telling us about faith and reason? Does faith operate on one side of my brain and reason on the other side of my brain? Or is faith a type of knowing that comes from loving. Wisdom! We know "that" but we hardly know "what." When reason begins to operate within the context of faith, we have something like the oil and the Kleenex. Are we doing what is natural to us, separating what we distinguish? We find it very difficult to distinguish without separating. But theologically we always have to ask that question. When we distinguish nature from grace, are we separating them automatically? And the answer very often is "no." We have to make that very clear to our theological thinking. Or it can become very muddled.

**Sollee:**   The subject of nature and grace or faith and reason, I believe is central to our topic today, especially the last phrase of our conference title: "The God Question." Although these subjects are usually relegated to the academy, they flesh themselves out in the every day life of the believer and nonbeliever. An even more poignant way to approach this is the "knowledge problem, or what Professor Steven L. Goldman has coined in his Teaching Company series: "Science Wars: What Scientists Know and How They Know It." Science has a temporal dimension and is a consensus world-view of its practitioners. It deals with secondary causes and never delivers finished truth statements. It can point to the Real but is impotent in giving us meaning, value and experience of the Real.

In Jacques Maritain's masterful book, *The Degrees of Knowledge*, he shows the progression or evolution of the human intellect from basic reason to the highest stages of spiritual knowledge. Also in Maritain's little book *Approaches to God*, he also shows how the natural intellect can be led to believe in the One Source. These two texts have led me, in some mysterious way, to remember that I have always been in the "mind of God." This I believe is the normal progression of grace perfecting nature. There most likely would not be a "God question," if one would stop the internal and external noise and listen to the small quiet voice within.

**Muller, Earl:**    Bringing in the whole issue of nature and grace and their insepa-rability touched on points that I had thought about before. One of the things that is not always adverted to in Thomas Aquinas' *Summa Theologica* is the question of the Incarnation and whether Christ would have been incarnate apart from the sin of Adam. Thomas says, no. But he answers an objection that the incarnation was revealed to Adam prior to his fall; and the point of the objection itself was that if Adam knew about the Incarnation before his fall, then his fall would not have been the cause for the Incarnation. The text that this argument focuses on is from Ephesians 5 where Paul refers to the Genesis text on the creation of the woman, "…and I'm saying this about Christ and the church." Thomas answers by saying that we can know an effect without knowing the cause. Adam could know the incarnation without knowing the cause of the incarnation, which is to say his own future sinfulness.

What Thomas is saying is that he accepts the basic presupposition that the cre-ation of the woman is the revelation of Christological structure, that male and female reveals Christ in the church. If we take this one step further, that Adam and Eve were already created in the image of Christ, this would also then imply that human rationality is best understood as that rationality which was assumed by Christ. As assumed by Christ, therefore, human rationality is graced even from the very beginning. One of the expectations is that rationality in Christ has an openness and orientation toward God the Father. This is presupposed by John Paul II in his Genesis catechesis. This openness to God is ingredient to who we are; it is ingredient within our rationality.

This openness to transcendence, of course, is precisely what allows us to move from the structures of our rationality, from the wonder that we experience, to an affirmation that there is something that corresponds to this. But of course this Christological structure of our humanity, and more particularly of our human rationality, can be rejected.

**Barr:**    This has to do with the comment made about the relationship between faith and reason which cannot be separated. They can in a sense. Also on the

92

comment made earlier by Francisco Muller: how some atheists don't have a realist physics so that they don't necessarily affirm that there is anything in reality. They say what's going on in our minds has no necessary correlation with reality outside

I think they may not have any good way of justifying this. If they were to ask themselves, "why is it that what is in my mind corresponds to what is out there;" they might be led away from atheism. But in fact maybe unthinkingly they do have a faith in reason. They do have confidence that the rational thought processes give them access to what is really out there and is true. People like Dawkins regard themselves as champions and Apostles of reason.

Implicit in that is a kind of a natural faith – a faith that there *are* answers. We have to have the kind of faith that there are answers. The scientist has a kind of implicit faith that there are answers to his questions. He doesn't know why something is true but he is convinced passionately that there is a rational explanation.

*l to r: Anne McGuire and Sr. Marcianne*

*Ben Abell, our meteorologist "par excellence"*

# Astronomy/Cosmology Breakthroughs and the God Question

## Session 3

*Proceedings of the ITEST Symposium - September, 2007*

**Streeter:**   I just want to offer another image. We're talking about faith and reason and so on. Something that sometimes helps with some of my students is that I simply ask them how many eyes they have in their head. And of course they think I'm joking because they all know that they have two eyes. And I ask them, if you see double where do you go? And they all laugh because they know that they'd have to visit the eye doctor. Well, then if you have no trouble knowing that you have two eyes in your head and you still have a singleness of vision, then maybe we can begin the understanding of how faith and reason can give us a whole unified view of life.

We have two eyes: we have faith and we have reason but they form a unified vision of a total reality, not two. You don't have one eyeball going this way and one eyeball going that way. So that is a helpful image which could be springboard into pondering it a little more deeply.

The other item I wanted to mention is something that maybe we can discuss with our atheistic scientists. Again I go along with some of the Lonergan insights. About 99 percent of our lives operate on belief, not knowledge. We have to believe that when we turn on the ignition in the car that the motor is going to kick in and go. Maybe I don't know how that motor works. We have to believe that there is only 10 percent ethanol in that gas tank when we fill up. How do we know? We read the label and we believe. This is purely human faith.

We believe that that red light is going to turn green and that the cars will stop. We believe that there is only 600 milligrams of salt in the pork and beans because the label says so. We believe the doctor who tells us why we have that skin rash. We have not scientifically verified that knowledge. We would be amazed if we were to go through our lives and really take stock of how much we live our entire life on human faith.

That's why we were so furious with Enron. After investing our money, our faith and even our children's future to them, they betrayed us. We believed in them on human faith. We didn't check out everything rationally making sure that we had all the knowledge we needed. Let's face it, much of our lives is lived on some kind of human belief.

This is a truth that, I don't think we allude to now. Maybe if we really sat down with some of our atheistic scientists and talked, they would have to face facts - just basic straight human facts.

**Muller, Earl:** This is just a brief follow-up to comments that Stephen Barr had finished with. This was to point out that when you look at *Dei Verbum* or at Vatican I, when they talk about the distinction between faith and revelation and reason, they are citing the first question of the Summa Theologica of Thomas. When you go there, it becomes clear that Revelation for Thomas equals the Scriptures. That leaves open the whole question of a natural revelation, a natural grace, as it were, whereby God is communicating himself. I think that kind of notion touches on what you were talking about, Dr. Barr, in terms of this more differentiated reality we see, for example, in how people are open – even atheists in some cases – to certain types of transcendence. Even the kind of a natural grace of revelation.

**Murphy, Mary Ellen:** I have a comment to add to what John Cross was saying early today about Teilhard and the fact that things were getting more complex. But I think that part of Teilhard's message was not only that they are getting more complex, but there is also a continued development of our consciousness and an ongoing development of the human race. But at the same time I think that he also said that we would be moving toward unity and that there would be more communication. We certainly see an awful lot more of communication in our day and age. In fact we are pretty much a global village at this point.

Secondly, I'd like to get back to the future! I'd like to talk about some of these exo-planets and the possibility of ones we haven't even seen yet that probably exist. Are they going to need a redeemer?

**Consolmagno:** There are two ways, both of them are possible. There is nothing in our theology of the redeemer that says it must be one way or the other. Is there an answer to the mocking question, "Does Christ have to die over and over again?" Christ dies over and over again millions of times every day in the sacrifice of the Mass. There is nothing out of line about that.

What do we know of the Redeemer, the Second Person of the Trinity, who was the Word who was there at the beginning, the one and the same at all places and at all times? I don't think we're going to have to have the Fourth, Fifth, Sixth and Seventh Person of the Blessed Trinity. That's not what is happening. Rather it is that the Word could be spoken in "other languages" to other creatures. If there are other planets, if there is a climate suitable for life, and so on, contributes to a long string of "if's." The most problematic is the concept that we could actually be in communication with other creatures, since every message about life would take 20 years to get here and 20 years to get back

Here is the difficulty of speaking across species. Every time the Church has had to deal with this issue in the past it's been with other human beings. And on the earth every human being can be traced back to a common ancestry. And it's never really been an issue. What the Redeemer would look like or even if one were needed for other creatures is a matter of science fiction. It is speculation. Rather than trying to come up with an answer, what I think is more fruitful is to say, "This is a wonderful way for us to contemplate what the Redemption actually means." I think it puts an entirely new light on what it meant for Christ to become a human being.

What does Christ's redemption mean in terms of dolphins, dogs, cats? What does the sin of Adam mean when we recognize the Adam story which is the underpinning of a lot of theology? This is not as straightforward history as many people thought years ago. And I don't have the answers to that. But I think what we do have is the opportunity to reflect on the questions in a different, richer way.

The most potent answer is the poem by Alice Meynell, *Christ in the Universe (1917)*, which says: if we could talk to those in the Pleiades, if we could talk to those in the constellation Taurus, they could tell us about the way the Redeemer came to them; so too we could tell them stories about the way the Redeemer came to us.

> But in the eternities,
> Doubtless we shall compare together, hear
> A million alien Gospels, in what guise
> He trod the Pleiades, the Lyre, the Bear
>
> O, be prepared, my soul!
> To read the inconceivable, to scan
> The myriad forms of God those stars unroll
> When, in our turn, we show to them a Man

We do know - it is part of our Faith - that we are not the only intelligent beings who are in a loving relationship with God. If we believe in anything, we can connect that with what we call Angels. Our tradition and the bible tell us that the Angels fell. It is a story similar to the Adam and Eve fall, but at the same time it was very different from the Adam and Eve story. That there was a deep fall, that there was a sin is true in both cases. But who's to say that a different race in a different place and a different time couldn't have a very different outcome that nonetheless involved the existence of the Second Person of the Blessed Trinity being present in creation there?

Having said all that, my last point is to remind you that these are not other heavens, these are not other worlds. This is all part of the same universe. If indeed there are other beings in that universe, they are not aliens. At most they are cousins. The redemptive act of Christ on earth is the redemptive act of the universe. Whether or not that act is spoken in a different language in a different place in a different time, we can't say. But certainly it is a redemptive act of the universe by Christ himself, as is every sacrifice of the Mass.

**Barr:** I was going to say that every time we sin we crucify Christ anew. Every time someone suffers, in the Body of Christ, Christ is suffering. Thomas Paine was wrong when he said that it was absurd to say that Christ dies over and over again. I strongly disagree with him. There is nothing absurd about Christ's dying over and over again - He does.

**Sollee:** The model I have is a cruciform A creation model. It says that we make up for the sufferings that are lacking in the body of Christ and then Christ does suffer with us. That old "pathos." Holmes Rolston put it together in that beautiful paper that I quoted at length in an earlier session. Christ constantly suffers with us.

**Consolmagno:** And if you want to play bible games with anyone who's trying to "throw curves at you," you can give them the Good Shepherd story from John, where in the end he says, "I have other sheep who are not in the fold..." (Laughter) that I also must go to."

**Muller, Francisco:** There are so many things I want to comment on, that it is difficult to put them together.

First, when you said that we have "more complexity and more unity," I want to believe it but, not necessarily complexity of beings redounds in unity. To achieve unity, complexity must be such as to reach "higher levels." Fr. Teilhard de Chardin put it nicely when he said: *"Everything that rises must converge."* So convergence, unification, communication, they all require a "rising" of existential levels. That is why mere information has not given us more communication. We have not risen to a community of hearts, of ideals, of values. Mere information has produced the opposite effect: a bigger pluralism of ideas, more fragmentation of society, where all is confused and "anything goes."

Commenting on what Brother Consolmagno said about a Redeemer. There is a theological opinion involved here. If extra-terrestrial life enjoys "free will" then those beings would certainly be morally responsible, whatever planet they inhabit. The question is: have they remained innocent or have they committed sin? Assuming the possibility that they have never committed sin then, a second question is: do they need a Redeemer? Do they need Christ? Here is where the mentioned theological opinion comes into play: it posits that Christ would have come, anyway, even if there had been no original sin. In that case He does not come to "repair" or "save" something, but simply to be the "culmination," the "crowning" of all Creation, the King of God's creatures. In that view Christ would not be Neyle's cruciform Christ.

**Sollee:**   A loving, redeeming Christ

**Muller, Francisco:**   Yes, a loving Christ, but even if he came "only" as a King he would be also loving. Some theologians are so convinced about this loving incarnate Christ, (even without original sin) that they describe the rebellion of the bad angels precisely as a trial they were subjected to, upon foreseeing God's incarnation. Lucifer and his followers could not tolerate it. To have to adore God incarnate as a mere man, lower than the angels, was too humiliating for them. It is as if God incarnated in the form of an animal, say an ant, and then we would have to adore that ant.

So if as some theologians say, Christ not necessarily had to come for sin; then those peoples in other parts of the Universe (or in other universes) who might have never sinned, would also receive the second Person of the Trinity as their King and crown of their own Creation. (They might not even be "humans" like us). In that eventuality we would have a cruciform Christ for us, but a non-cruciform Christ for them. This would limit the cruciform, "kenotic" Christ just to the human race. I know this would go against much of Hegel's theology, in which God's incarnation and even the act of Creation is seen as a "kenosis" not only of the Son but also of the Father. In fact, as involving the whole Trinity, which agrees with Neyle's kenotic and cruciform Christ taken as a Universal fact, more Universal than in the previous hypothesis of "innocent" aliens not needing a cruciform Christ.

In favor of Hegel's and Neyle's idea, of the universality of original sin, I mean, of the cosmic resonance of our human fall, we have the mysterious text of St. Paul about the whole of Creation being subjected to the vanity of sin. *"From the beginning till now the entire creation, as we know, has been groaning in one great act of giving birth; and not only creation, but all of us who possess the first-fruits of the Spirit, we too groan inwardly as we wait for our bodies to be set free.*" (Romans 8). Of course I have no authority to interpret this "cosmo-theological" text of St. Paul, rarely studied by theologians, but as a philosopher I can suggest that the "entire creation" of St. Paul might be just "our Universe," in the physical sense of the word, and not any other unimaginable "universes" where morally responsible beings might exist. In that case they might not need the cruciform Christ, without denying the universality of God the Son as author of all that exists, even other universes.

A crucial problem here is what to understand by the word "Universe." String theorists, for example, are playing now with the idea of "multiverses" and eleven dimensions, etc. But we know they are talking of mere mathematical abstractions without even the hope of contacting our singular experimental world. Ontologically speaking there can be only "one" universe, since *all is being*, whatever the essence or modalities of those beings. But physically speaking, if we understand physics as everything that is like certain bodies, and can be related only to those certain bodies, then there could be "separation" of different universes, one for each type of physical bodies or entities. We know at least that the glorified body of the resurrected Christ is not subjected to the physical laws of "our universe." He can come and go through the walls, just like X-rays do. He can be in several places at the same time, as in the consecrated hosts, (and even as some saints that miraculously have been bi-located)

In other words, separation of various universes means that they are not causally connected, not even by the relationships of distance, much less of "light" propagation. It is a very unfortunate twist of contemporary physics to imagine that the basic causal connection between bodies is by light signals. Prior to light travel there exists the distance between bodies, which distance is, itself, a causal connection. Eliminate this profound causal connectivity and you don't have even "space." That is why "heaven" is not "here" or "there" because it is not spatially or causally related to us. As in the parable of Lazarus and the rich man, there is an "abyss" between the final states of both men, as described by Abraham.

Summarizing therefore: Just as God created the angelic essences in a spiritual universe totally diverse from ours, He could have created other physical universes including intelligent free beings, diverse from ours in the sense of being non-causally connected, hence having no distance, no communicability, no reciprocal influence with us. In that case those moral and intelligent beings could either, (1) have remained innocent, in which case the Son would crown "their" universe, just as He will crown ours, but without the convenient bloody redemption. Or, (2) if they had sinned, then, yes, they would need a kenotic Christ, after the manner of their own physical essence.

The difficulty (and also interesting aspect) starts when we imagine intelligent beings *within* our physical universe and, hence, potentially communicating and interacting with us. The dilemmatic hypothesis of their being innocent or being sinful also takes place, again leading to the two possible consequences of a triumphant kingly Christ, or a kenotically saving one for them. In all cases the whole of Creation is One, ontologically speaking, as One is the Christ that by way of "incarnation" (suffering or not) "recapitulates" the whole of the Universe(s) for God in each of God's creatures. But Paul's phrase of the "whole of creation groaning" still points to a universally sinful condition, specially for those aliens that could inhabit our universe. Such is, indeed, the "connectivity" of the cosmos even (and specially) from a spiritual point of view. This physical connectivity is what produces the "transmission" of original sin from Adam and Eve to us, just by procreation. But also this physical connectivity is what saves us, when the new Adam took our humanity from the new Eve, and died for us on the cross. Since those possible aliens are certainly not connected to us by procreation their status as sinful or not cannot be decided by theological necessity. I leave that question open, but we cannot, *a priori*, judge them sinful and needing redemption.

**Muenck:** I have two points. The line from the Bible "I make up for what is lacking in the sufferings of Christ." I know that that one is commonly misunderstood. The only thing Christ is lacking is my participation. He can't save me without my cooperation.

The second point is another clarification: the Church teaches that Christ died only once and every time we offer the sacrifice of the Mass, we mystically go back to that point in time. That being so, it would be illogical for Christ to have died again in other worlds. Therefore if there are aliens in other worlds, we would be charged to bring Christ to those others.

**Barr:** Let me comment on that last one, if I may. It seems to me that the traditional view is that originally there was a unity at the human race which was destroyed by Original Sin. And that Christ is restoring the human race – He is the New Adam – but it is the human race. The church is the mystical body of Christ, but that is a human body. If there were 50 different species out there, though rational, free with immortal souls and so on, they too would need to be united to God in some mystical body as a distinct species. They are not trace-able to Adam, not biologically connected to us human beings. That would be a different body of Christ. Christ assumed a human nature here, and there will be a human mystical body.

But the Second Person of the Trinity could assume another nature — maybe an octopus, I don't know. Some other rational beings with their own distinctive na-ture. We can assume that. And those beings would be united with God in a body but it wouldn't be the same one as ours. It would be kind of an inter-species, whatever we would call it. There wouldn't be that original unity between their species and ours. We couldn't incorporate them into our church because we are a different body so to speak, a different flock.

I'm not sure, Francisco (Muller), that I agree with your logic on your last point. There wouldn't be a sort of universal church in that sense, a cosmic church of many different species from many different worlds.

**Sollee:** Also, on the suffering Christ – I haven't talked to God lately but I'm open to the thought of Christ suffering in me, and it is one of the possibilities of my spiritual growth and development. I really don't have to be right or wrong; I can hold that position until I mature one way or the other. I don't think it will affect my salvation one way or the other if I think Christ suffered or not. But I think it can help me if I can presume that He is suffering because that gives me a tension right there and it makes me work at it. There is such a thing as the Holy Spirit teaching us. St Paul says that we will be taught by the Holy Spirit and not by anyone else. If we believe that, then we need to stay tuned in and walk upright in grace. We need to become holy, and do as St Paul says, "Be crucified with Christ…" by duplicating his type of death. We gain eternal life by knowing and loving Christ.

**Muller, Earl:** My two points are about Thomas Aquinas. The first comment I almost sort of dismiss because by the time Guy had finished talking, he had cov-ered most of the points that I was going to make. But this is about the angels and about the unfallen angels. In the *Summa* Thomas asks whether Christ is the Head of the Angels. And he answers positively, "Yes." I'm referring to what Stephen Barr said about other races being other bodies – you can also understand other races as having a purely natural destiny as opposed to having a supernatural des-tiny. St Paul was saying that if other alien races have a supernatural destiny, it is because of what Christ did here. In Heaven they would be incorporated into the one city of God because there is only one city of God.

The other point is a correction of what Francisco Muller said – that Thomas Aquinas would have held that there would have been an incarnation anyway. That's not the case. Thomas was aware that that is an opinion that is being voiced by other medieval theologians and he expressly rejects it and cites two main reasons for it: the testimony of Scripture which always links the Incarnation to the sin of Adam. But then also the liturgy – the Easter Vigil: "O happy fault that merited so great a Redeemer." So Thomas is negative on that point. But there are medieval theologians who do support it, John Duns Scotus, for instance and probably the Franciscans in general. You'll find lots of modern theologians willing to assume that position.

**Kuhl:** I wanted to comment on the point that Fr. Muller made regarding Thomas Aquinas and the debate in the Middle Ages. Is Christ really a principle of God coming into the world to bring to fulfillment what we were intended to be in creation? In Eastern theology that is prevalent with the Eastern Fathers. And they don't have a doctrine of Original Sin.

In the West there was predominantly the understanding that it is because of sin that Christ came and that Redemption has to do with death and resurrection, that is to say, the old passes away. All things become new. So Christ's death and resurrection is, if you will, the archetype that all of us experience through union with Christ. That is a very important theological notion. I think it's a question that sometimes gets raised when we're discussing cosmology and maybe astrophysics. What does this kind of sense mean that is associated with the Christian as passing away from the old and the coming of a new creation? We are a new creation in Christ. That is precisely Paul's way of describing it. This isn't simply leaving this place and going to Heaven. In Romans 8 Paul describes it:

> I consider that the sufferings of this present time can not compare with the glory to be revealed to us. For the creation waits with eager longing for the revealing of the children of God. For the creation was subjected to futility not of its own will but by the will of the one who subjected it in order that the creation itself would be set free from the bondage to decay and will obtain the freedom of the glory of the children of God. We know that the whole creation has been groaning in labor pains until now; and not only the creation but we ourselves who have the first fruits of the Spirit, groan inwardly as we wait for our bodies to be set free.

That is at the heart, core and center of soteriology salvation, the resurrection.

Theology asks, if there is any evidence of this world being in bondage because of human sin itself and under decay. Is this whole cosmos, this whole world dependent upon this human steward who sinned and destroyed the integrity of the world? Now can this beginning in connection with Christ be the vehicle by which the whole creation looks forward to its redemption? Do cosmologists think in those terms or talk in those terms? It is certainly the eschatology of the new testament and the resurrection of the body. Is this the reason why God is important for cosmologists as they approach these limit factors or these anthropic coincidences?

**Consolmagno:**   I had a nice glib answer ready for you which I already built a counter argument to. The interesting thing to me is a statement I made that we don't actually know whether it's true. How many images are there in the universe? 50,000, 100,000? Have you ever seen an ugly image of space taken through a telescope?

Ugliness to our eyes is associated truly with human sin. All ugliness is related to sin. On the other hand I've seen some pretty good looking sinners.

The counter example of course is that, seen from the moon, the Earth is a very beautiful place. So, if there were sin elsewhere it would be on a scale we couldn't measure.

**Pouch:**   We keep coming back to the questions of anthropic arguments or anthropic coincidences.

I have a science fiction story by Poul Anderson with the title, "Details"[1] From the story, I'll quote the thoughts of KRI, their highest official:

> So many planets, spinning through night and cold, so many souls, huddled on them... a half-million full-status worlds, near galactic center, members of interstellar civilization by virtue of knowing that such a civilization existed... and how many millions more who did not know? It seemed that every day a scoutship brought back word of yet another inhabited planet.

[1] (Worlds of IF, Oct. 1956, reprinted in *Seven Conquests*, copyright 1984 by Baen Enterprise, p. 146 [ISBN 0-671-55914-1]). The story concerns an outpost on Earth from an interstellar League composed entirely of humans.

106

Each of them had its human races – red, black, white, yellow, blue, green, brown; tall or short; thin or fat; hairy or bald; tailed or tailless; but fully human, biologically human, and the scientists had never discovered why evolution should work thus on every terrestroid world. The churches said it was the will of the Designer, and perhaps they were right. Certainly they were right in a pragmatic sense, for the knowledge had brought the concept of brotherhood and duty. The duty of true civilization was to guide its brothers in darkness – secretly, gently, keeping them from the devastating knowledge that a million-year-old society already existed, until they had matured enough to take that bitter pill and join smoothly the League of the older planets.

The problem with any anthropic argument is that you will have some determined doubters who will not be convinced by any coincidence, no matter how big, and will persist in doubt or disbelief. Nor will there be a materialist explanation of some event strong enough to shatter a person's faith, if they are of great faith. You're not going to win one way or the other.

I'd like to build on Guy's theme that science doesn't *prove* things: all you ever get in science is that this or that theory is *consistent with* some set of observations. You want your theory to be *consistent with* as large a set of observations as possible. Another thing you want from scientific theory is not only that it be consistent with what you *do* observe, but you kind of like it to be inconsistent with what you *don't* observe, or better still, with what you observe to not happen. You would like your theory of the origin of Earth's moon to explain not only why the *one* moon formed, but why it didn't form into six equally-spaced smaller moons, or a solid band, or other things that aren't there.

In geology, we like plate tectonics, because it not only explains where volcanoes *do* occur, but also where they *don't* occur; plate tectonics explains fairly well where earthquakes occur, with the glaring exception of New Madrid, Missouri, and explains fairly well where they don't occur.

From science, you won't get proof that God exists, or is benign, or any other article of the Creed, simply because science as such doesn't provide what a philosopher or mathematician would consider proofs. What we can do is show that a loving God is consistent with the universe that we see as we see it. You can't possibly do better than that, and you probably can't do worse than that, but that last is more of a faith-statement.

I'd like to build on Stephen Barr's Science-Building-Downward analogy and issue a warning to theologians and apologists. Building-downward is how science really works. Basically, we start off with a ridiculously large number of laws and observations dealing with particular special cases, and, as time goes by, and if we are lucky, we end up with a smaller number of laws that cover more general cases. The problem is that all of our special cases don't turn out the way we hoped. The reason you don't start a building by constructing and furnishing the first floor and later installing a foundation is that Bad Things happen when you do it this way.

The Galileo crisis is a good example of that. We had built a lot of theology around earlier "science." The one thing I can guarantee about science is that it *will move*, and it will crack and break things built around it. Science will move on: that is in its nature. One of the problems we can run into is that by making faulty arguments that reach a true or even True, conclusion, we cast the conclusion into doubt when the argument is at fault. For example, I can argue that diamonds are made from subjecting coal to high pressure and that therefore the presence of diamonds shows the existence of high-pressure conditions, but when it becomes clear diamonds are not formed from metamorphism of coal, it can cast doubt on the existence of high pressure metamorphism, even if high pressure metamorphism does occur.

We, as church, do need to respond to arguments against the existence of God based on science, but it is really not a good idea to put a lot of effort into arguments like " A balances B: therefore, God must exist."

**Mahfood:**   I want to start off by saying that this has been an incredibly fascinating bit of speculation what Heaven will look like if we get there – whether or not there will be "all of us" present with a lot of other creatures. If there is a single Kingdom of God, and that's what we believe, because God is One, and that Heaven is a total communion with God, then we will be in total communion with each other when we are in Heaven. I'm just going by analogy of the idea of our eternal destiny in the sweetness and love of God's presence. So that would imply that, along with every other being that has a supernatural destiny, (as Steve argued earlier) we would be in communion with them as well. So it wouldn't matter what race: human or non-human. Even in our resurrected bodies we would be in full communion.

So this leads me to another bit of speculation. In Revelation John sees these interesting creatures in attendance, in their various activities. Are these other supernatural creatures that at one time had incarnate bodies on other planets? The idea of anthropic coincidence has also left me with another question. Christ had a human body and he took it with Him. So wherever that is, He is still present in his Human body. So if that is the case, we know that he is not going to take on the body of an octopus, for instance, Well, what's he going to do with his human body?

**Barr:**   What's to prevent him from having more than one body?

**Mahfood:**   He could have the body of a human and the body of an octopus, maybe. My point is this: if they are all in communion in Heaven then it is possible, it seems to me that we would be able to translate the Gospel message to those we encounter in other places. Because they would have the same supernatural destiny that we have, they would be perceptive to hearing that through whatever process of inculteration, we would encounter.

**Barr:**   I agree with what you say; I think it is dangerous to try to build too much theology on the foundations of science. There is a connection here with Michael Heller (mentioned earlier) who has some very interesting things to say in his book, *Creative Tension.*[2] He talks about how it is unavoidable that Christians in any era are going to have a kind of -- I'm not sure exactly what he calls it – a world image or a world.

**Pouch:**   Let's call it a paradigm or worldview.

**Barr:**   But it's not theology so much; it's a way of looking at the world that integrates their religious beliefs with their casual knowledge of the world – more of a picture that they have of the world. And it is inevitable that Medievals should strive for a coherent view of the world, which would incorporate their Christian faith, the science of the day and the common sense of their day.

But we should always recognize that the ideas of the times change; the science changes. That's necessary – it shifts. So one doesn't want to get one's theology too deeply interwoven with the ideas of time because when time and other ideas start shifting, your theology can get in trouble.

So, my view is: what makes natural theologies part of this? They should be *robust*, of a kind that are not going to be affected by future scientific developments.

---

[2] Michael Heller, *Creative Tension: Essays on Science and Religion* (Philadelphia and London: Templeton Foundation Press, 2003).

One of the classical traditional arguments that have been made in the book of Wisdom, and by the early Apologists, was based simply on the providence, order and law – the mere fact that the world is orderly, that it's beautiful.

Now if we take a look at some scientific knowledge or theory (whether it's super string theory or something else), history has shown that we'll see a world that is more orderly than we imagined, more beautiful. So, those kinds of arguments are *robust*. But if you start making theological arguments based on a particular theory (as some of the intelligent design proponents do) you are asking for trouble. Because when the scientific theory changes, your theological argument collapses; and this creates a tremendous problem for everyone. So natural theology can be done as long as it's done in terms of the various *robust* features of the world that aren't vulnerable to those kinds of scientific progress.

**Sheahen:** I'm reminded by Stephen's last statement about a line that is quoted from St. Augustine in Guy Consolmagno's paper about how it is embarrassing when a Christian speaks in a way that is known to other people to be obviously ridiculous. I don't know if I quoted Augustine accurately there but that is certainly the general idea.

**Consolmagno:** The special irony of course is that "everyone knows," that Augustine is referring to, is the Ptolemaic astronomy – which we now know is false. Nonetheless, the point is a valid one.

**Pouch:** When making natural theology arguments the problem is *a priori* knowing what is a "robust argument that will be invariant under all possible transformations." As Guy pointed out: "Sure, everyone knows that the Earth is a sphere at the center of a series of concentric spheres with things rotating around other things." But when that "certainty" [Ptolemaic astronomy] fell apart, it caused a lot of trouble for theology which had been built around it, and we wound up with the Galileo crisis, and theologians now rightly want to avoid making that same mistake.

But we do have to make natural theology arguments (to teach in terms of familiar concrete, ordinary situations) to be effective. One of the things that is most striking when you read the Gospels, followed immediately by a letter of Paul or any academic writings, is that Jesus made an awful lot of arguments that sound like "Look, the Kingdom of God is like farming, in that you sow seed, only some of which takes root and produces well, but *that* seed produces very well." Or "The Kingdom of God is like a mustard seed which is the smallest seed but begets a big plant." In other words, Jesus taught with familiar, concrete examples, and it worked quite well: it's not as effective to teach with abstract arguments of abstract terms. The problem with natural theology arguments is that you don't know beforehand what's going to come back and bite you, so I have some suggestions.

As Church, we do have to make natural law theological arguments, so that people understand them. But, building on Stephen Barr's Science-building-downward analogy, I'd suggest the following:

1. One of the points of an organization like ITEST is to give warning of where and when construction will happen, so we can try to gracefully evacuate the rooms that will be affected beforehand.

2. Another is that when you get involved in natural law theology arguments, have some back-up arguments, so that if one of them fails, you have something else to fall back on.

3. The third is, when you are making a natural theology argument, to make it clear that 'this is the best way I can explain it to you', as opposed to 'this is what Scripture teaches or this is what the Catholic Church has, (and always will) held as being the truth'.

A lot of problems arise from people attaching far too much authority to something that was a very good analogy when it was made, but after a few hundred years pass, and our understanding has changed, the analogy falls apart on you, even though the original understanding is still quite reasonable. For example, likening the Kingdom of God to a mustard seed (Matthew 13:31-32) is still true whether there are seeds smaller than that of a mustard plant, but it is easy to obsess on such issues.

**Kappes:**   One of the reasons I came to this conference was, I love astronomy. I can remember years ago, particles traveling through Earth's atmosphere and instead of growing older, they grew younger.

**Consolmagno:**   I think you are referring to particles that were decaying slower than they should have because they were traveling across a longer distance – muons

**Kappes:**   I imagined that we would be hearing the latest from the world, the voice of astronomy on time – time warps!! What's new? What's been discovered? Wormholes. Time Alteration? What are they calling it all? Then I'm interested in how that intersects with the reports about the experience of mystics who describe states in which time is altered. What's going on? What is the latest from the world of astronomy on time?

**Barr:**   The latest would be Einstein's theory of general relativity which describes the structure of space and time. There's nothing really new in a sense at least for the last 91 years or so. (1916)

**Kappes:**   Did String Theory have anything to do with that?

**Barr:**   Most people in particle physics expect that general relativity, Einstein's theory of space and time, has a deeper theory underlying it. Most of the people think that it is something like String Theory, but that's still very speculative; nobody knows. And at the moment general relativity works very well. It's what we have and some people think that it's a manifestation of something else. The idea that a lot of people have is that in the ultimate theory – if we ever have it – and understand it – we'll find that our concepts of space and time will turn out to be approximations, just useful approximations. For example if you look at things at very short distances, our very notions of space and time will break down.

But we don't know exactly. We don't know what the next theory will do. So we can say that nothing new has happened. But I think there is a theological lesson to learn. Michael Heller talks a lot about time, what we've learned about time and its theological implications. This is his specialty; Heller is a relativist – he comments on relativity and quantum cosmology and so on. I recommend that you read some of his books.

I do think there's a lesson that physics' ideas of time have for theology. There are theologies that would like to embed God, the divine nature, more in time – I'm talking about the human nature of Christ here. One example would be the *open theisms*, I think they are called , according to which God, in his divine knowledge, does not know the future. Or some radical versions of *Kenotic theology* say that God emptied himself not only in the Incarnation, taking the form of a slave, but that the divine knowledge somehow became less – that the Second Person of the Trinity even in His Divine nature somehow emptied himself and ceased to be God. Thus there are some radical versions of kenotic theology which make the divine nature change in time. All of those ideas create problems .

When you start embedding God into time and space you are starting to put him down on the level of the "created," the creature. Then the problem arises that what we learned about time and space may not be consistent with what these theologies are positing. From the point of view of modern physics, those theologies have severe difficulties. The traditional Augustinian view of God outside of time, as timeless, comports very well with modern ideas about the nature of time. The more new-fangled theologies have some severe problems of consistency with modern physics.

**Kappes:**   What do you think Prigogene is doing with time?

**Barr:**   I don't know anything about him.

**Consolmagno:**   And I know even less. Michael Heller has been mentioned a number of times. He has spent a lot of time working with the Vatican Observatory and so I know him pretty well. In fact when I was giving a talk in Cracow, and he was present, he simultaneously translated into Polish while I was lecturing. I noticed that half the audience would laugh when I told a joke and then he would translate it into Polish, and the other half would laugh.

When I first met Michael Heller, he was in Tucson for a heart operation. Poland had just come from behind the Iron Curtain. Since there weren't many good hospitals in Poland, we paid for him to get the operation in the United States. Before his surgery we took him out to dinner. Being a young astronomer then, I was ignorant of his credentials. I said to him, "Oh, Michael Heller; what do you do?" And over dinner he explained what he did. It was an exceedingly humiliating experience for me – humbling would be a better word – but for me it was humiliating. For me to realize with my theology degree and all my education that I understood about one word in ten of what he was saying. His books are not easy to read, but I would certainly recommend them to you.

On the nature of time in general the big insight came while I was teaching in Kenya for two years in the Peace Corps, teaching physics to university people. I had an odd experience. If I had a free day I'd spend it giving my physics students the outlines of relativity theory. In relativity theory usually things shrink and mass grows and things go as fast as the speed of light – all these paradoxes. But all my students in Africa sat there and said, "Whatever the professor says must be true…" And I was trying to get them to be amazed. So finally I thought, "I'll give them the famous twin paradox – where one twin stays home and the other flies off into space in a high-speed rocket.[3] Remember I was teaching in Africa in 1984 -- "OK, let's pretend it's 1994," I said to the students, and I wrote on the board, "Here in 1994 I'm building a space shuttle." The entire class broke out laughing at the concept of pretending that it was a different year than the year it actually was. That was the most amazing thing they had heard me say.

I later talked to people who worked in African theology and philosophy. They said that our idea of time is a line which we have so embedded in us that we take it for granted and that learning relativity is really kind of scary when we realize that the line shifts as you change your speed. That is a very modern, western artificial concept. The African concept is that time consists of two locations. There is the forever "Now" and there is the historical "Then." And old people are greatly valued because they have traveled from the "Then" place to the 'Now" place. But the culture lives in the eternal "now" which is why you can't tell them if you leave the water faucet open today you'll have no water tomorrow because that kind of causality isn't part of the culture. To realize that makes us understand that our current idea of time – which we think is so "common-sensical" is also in many ways a convention. It is a useful convention and allows us to do lots of good things, but it is still a convention.

**Sheahen:** With regard to what Guy has just talked about, I am one nut who wants to go around calling time a complex variable. It isn't just a line; it is not just a one- dimensional real axis; it's a plane. Particular values of time are places out on the plane which, if you could only have access to it, would allow you to go back and forth. You'd be able to travel around in that complex plane. However, that can only be labeled speculation and not promoted seriously.

**Kuhl:** In my paper I raised the idea from the Encyclopedia of Philosophy that cosmology, that term or that discipline, has two sub-groups: a philosophical one and a scientific one. I don't understand those two different sub-groups and how they may be related to one another. If someone could explain that to me, that would be helpful. Also, can you discuss the kind of debate (like the one we're having) with regard to theology and astro-physics. What happens within cosmology with regard to the grounding, the foundation – what makes the whole make sense? Is that too much to put on the floor at this time of the evening or should we save it for the next session?

---

[3] *(When the "flying" twin returns to Earth he finds that he has aged less than the twin who stayed on Earth. The apparent contradiction is explained within the framework of relativity theory. [Editors])*

# Astronomy/Cosmology Breakthroughs and the God Question

## Session 4

*Proceedings of the ITEST Symposium - September, 2007*

**Sheahen:** I think we need a little perspective about the probability of their being other "beings" or aliens in the universe. There is a book entitled, "Are We Alone in the Universe?" that explores the question. But the idea that we *are* alone in the universe is definitely a possibility. The "anthropic coincidences" we've spoken of are a collection of numerical ratios that are fine-tuned to about one part in $10^{120}$ or perhaps one in $10^{500}$. As Stephen Barr said yesterday morning, it's a slam dunk when you first look at it that God designed this universe. And it is pretty convincing. Remember, the only way to dismiss that evidence is to go down the route of *multiverses*. But remember, in the *multiverses* all the other "multi's" are unobservable by us. So any interaction with these "beings" on other planets won't happen outside the known Universe. And as a result, we earthlings probably aren't going to have much interaction. So the question of the redemption-need by the people on other planets is a slightly empty question.

One thing to remember is this: we exist in a small slice of time. The Sun is a second generation star, formed from the dust and gas of earlier stars that blew up. It might have taken about 8 billion years after the big bang. Now, consider another galaxy, another star, where that same procedure is followed. But suppose we're 5.0 billion years old and they're 5.1 billion year old — that's a pretty small margin. Well, folks, we missed them by a hundred million years, which puts us back in the dinosaur time when they're out looking for us. That's three orders of magnitude longer than the evolution of mankind; four orders of magnitude longer than any semblance of recorded history; six orders of magnitude longer than the time we've had radio waves. So the likely overlap with an alternative civilization, in this or in any other galaxy in the universe, has a diminishing small probability.

Continuing that same thought, the first speaker this morning is:

**Abell:** Are There Other Civilizations?

Are they like us or not like us in appearance? I can accept either scenario. Two of the essayists briefly mentioned what a remarkable place this earth is. We have a temperature range from forty degrees below zero Celsius to about forty degrees above zero Celsius, but other unique features are present, and I would like to address them.

*(The editors chose to highlight the following intervention on climate and weather because it is an important document in itself and makes a significant contribution to the proceedings of the symposium. Rather than excise it from the discussion session and place it as an appendix, the editors decided to set it off from the rest of the text so that the reader could note it as a research piece worthy of deeper study.)*

**Abell:**  When I refer to the earth-atmosphere system, I include the region from the earth to the top of the atmosphere. The rotation of the earth and the geometry of the earth's movement around the sun must also be considered. Radiative energy is both entering and exiting the atmosphere at the top of the earth-atmosphere system. There are other energy exchanges, but they are minute. Short wave solar radiation enters the atmosphere. Thirty percent is returned immediately to space as albedo (combination of reflected and back scattered solar radiation). The remainder heats the earth-atmosphere-system, which in turn radiates in the long wave-length spectrum determined by the temperature of the radiating material. This is an extremely complex problem which yields to a solution using the laws of physics and mathematics.

There is an energy balance at the top of the earth's atmosphere where incoming solar radiation is nearly equal to the albedo plus returning terrestrial long wave radiation. This is not the case at the surface of the earth. Only about half of the incoming solar radiation is absorbed by the earth's surface. The remainder is depleted by the reflected and back scattered solar radiation as well as absorption by atmospheric gases and clouds. The earth and atmosphere then reradiate in the long wave spectrum. Since the atmospheric gases reradiate in all directions, there is a radiative imbalance at the earth's surface. The earth's outgoing radiation is only about half the radiation absorbed by the earth, yet the energy exchange must be nearly equal.

Mixing in the atmosphere (turbulence) helps to maintain the energy balance, but the large contributor to the energy balance at the earth's surface is through the evaporation-condensation cycle. Water evaporated from the earth's surface (including the seas) carries heat away from the surface. This heat is released into the atmosphere when water vapor condenses to form clouds. Precipitation from clouds returns water to the earth. This mechanism is the great energy equalizer. It is enormous. Again, this demonstrates that the earth and its atmosphere are remarkable.

If you experiment with a cloud chamber where the air inside is mostly clear of impurities, condensation (cloud) will not form until the relative humidity approaches several hundred percent. The maximum value of relative humidity in the atmosphere is one hundred percent. However the real atmosphere is dirty. It contains a number of impurities on which water vapor condenses as the relative humidity approaches one hundred percent. The nuclei include salt mostly derived from the seas, earth particles raised by the wind, and pollutants from industry and combustion. These particles will moisten and become water droplets when air is cooled and/or existing water droplets advect into a region. The most efficient method for cooling air is rapid ascent. This may be accomplished by wind moving air over rising terrain, by frontal lifting and by other dynamic mechanisms. As these mechanisms continue, clouds develop, but clouds do not guarantee precipitation.

How many times have you observed clouds which do not precipitate? Something else is necessary. Once again nature provides us with answers to our problem. At temperatures less than freezing, cloud droplets and drops can exist in the liquid state. This is referred to as supercooled water. If an object such as an aircraft enters this environment, the air craft structures will immediately acquire an ice coating. If the environment remains undisturbed, there will be a mixture of water drops and ice crystals if temperatures are cool enough. The water drops evaporate and the additional vapor will crystallize on the existing ice crystals. The resulting snow crystals continue to grow until they fall through the rising air reaching the earth as snow or rain (melted snow) as they fall through warmer air.

Suppose the rising air is not cool enough to produce ice crystals? During World War II, aviators noticed rain falling from clouds where temperature throughout the clouds was greater than freezing. This is often the case in the tropics and even in middle latitudes and at times in polar latitudes in the warm seasons. In these situations, rising impurities of different sizes and weights rise at different speeds as water vapor condenses on them. Since the growing drops rise at different rates, slower drops and faster drops contact one another and coalesce becoming large enough to fall toward earth as rain. Again, our earth-atmosphere system is unique.

Let us briefly return to the energy balance. The remarks to this point refer to the balance averaged over many seasons and years over all latitudes. There is still a problem because tropical and subtropical regions would continue to warm while polar latitudes continue to cool, producing a heat surplus in one area and a heat deficit in another. The answer to this problem is wind, which distributes warmer air poleward and cooler air equatorward. Moving high and low pressure systems and their associated cold and warm fronts accomplish this. Another mechanism effective over large regions is the monsoon. The monsoon is a direct thermal circulation of a seasonal nature controlled by low pressure over middle and low latitudes in the warm season and by high pressure over middle and high latitudes in the cool season.

Eight thousand years ago, the earth was warmer than it is now. A cold period followed with renewed warming centered around 1000 A.D. This was followed by the Little Ice Age (1430-1850) despite the emergence of the Industrial Revolution. Global climate change has existed throughout earth history and this will continue.

Northern Europeans colonized Iceland, Greenland, and the Canadian Maritimes during the warm period centered around 1000 A.D. Glaciers were retreating and Northern Hemisphere sea ice was greatly reduced. The Little Ice Age followed. Glaciers once again advanced and sea ice prevented ships from supplying Greenland. The colony was lost, but Iceland survived because ships were able to reach its shores during the warm season.

Global change continues. I question the accuracy of the climatology particularly over Southern Hemisphere seas. Reliable remote sensing of temperature dates only to modern satellite technology. I do agree that the earth is currently warming. The Little Ice Age ended only one hundred fifty years ago. The temperature increase is caused both naturally and anthroprogenically. The questions as to how much of the warming is due to nature and how much is human caused cannot be answered at this time. Obviously the increase in greenhouse gases will produce warming, but particulate pollution (smoke) counters some of the warming by raising the earth's albedo. Another factor is our variable star, the sun.

Radiation from the sun increases and decreases in a series of interacting cycles ranging from one hundred thousand years to eleven years. There is much to be learned. In the meantime, one answer is stewardship and its resulting implications.

Yes, the earth is indeed a unique and precious place.

---

**Mc Namara:** It seems to me that maybe you are turning the conversation in the direction which is re-focusing the original symposium question of God. The question of God for most of the world, as you said, is not the question of whether God exists or not; it's the question of — what you said earlier about stewardship. Why are those people living in those situations when they should be living in a better situation? As you said, most of the energy goes to the middle latitudes. So, what about the people in the Tropics? The people in the North?

One of our faculty just returned from a visit with the Inuits in Northern Canada. They are very much in a similar situation, socially speaking, as other peoples in developing countries. So the question of God for most of the world is, given that God exists, why are we in this particular situation? That takes us back to a consideration of the problem of evil. Don't we, as scientists have any responsibility to be stewards? That's what we are trying to do in our situation in the observatory in Manila in the Philippines. We are trying to make people aware that they don't have to just sit back and worry about the next typhoon or the next monsoon, earthquake, volcano eruption — all of which we have. Science can help them understand, first of all, that there is a way to get some rationality, if you will, to these things. These are energy sources, as you said. And eventually I think that human beings will learn how to tap those energies — say for geothermal energy – using the heat of the earth as a source for electricity.

**Muller, Francisco:** I would like to answer the question that Steve Kuhl formulated last night about the difference between scientific cosmology and philosophic cosmology. To answer this question I will refer to the insights of Jacques Maritain, the famous Catholic philosopher of the 20th century. He uses the three levels or degrees of abstraction: the physical, the mathematical and the philosophical abstraction, each one more abstract than the other, that is, the physical level at the first or lowest level and the philosophical at the third or highest level, with mathematics in between. Then he sees Mathematical Physics as the combination of the physical with the mathematical level (what the ancients called a *scientia* media). And he sees Philosophical Physics as the combination of the physical level with the philosophical level. This is what Aristotle did in his books of Physics, a truly philosophical physics. On the other hand Mathematical Physics started in the 17ᵗʰ century with Galileo and Newton. The latter's book, *Principia Matematica Philosophiae Naturalis* founded, as we know, Mathematical Physics, although it was called "natural philosophy" by most of Newton's contemporaries and even all the way to the 19ᵗʰ century. But a true "natural philosophy" must be a philosophical physics. Maritain uses the expression "Philosophy of Nature" for this physics, whereas the Catholic American philosopher Vincent Edward Smith calls it simply, Philosophical Physics. You can use either expression.

So what is the basic difference between Philosophical Physics and Mathematical Physics? Materially speaking they refer to exactly the same world, this Universe of ours. But formally speaking they differ in the interpretation they make of that same world. In Mathematical Physics we describe and explain physical bodies and their properties in terms of measurements, that is, numbers, and then we create a network of mathematical equations and theories to understand (or calculate) and predict that world. In Philosophical Physics we do not use numbers that much, we simply *read* or interpret the physical world in terms of being, nature, motion, substance, accident, cause, finality, matter, form, quality, alteration, mutation, time and space — that is, all the concepts developed by Aristotle in his Physics and later reformulated by Aquinas and most Scholastic philosophers. Are both types of knowledge compatible? Certainly yes. They can (and must) be integrated, uniting them but without confusing one type with the other.

The drama of the Galileo affair, the real drama, was that the old philosophers and theologians did not recognize that Galileo's (and, later, Newton's) Mathematical Physics was a totally new science. At the same time, Galileo and Newton and the founding fathers of that new Science, in general, did not recognize the perennial validity and truth of the older Philosophical or Aristotelian Physics. Because of some obsolete tenets of Aristotle's cosmology (like the heavenly spheres, the unequal fall of bodies, the distinction between celestial and terrestrial physics, etc), which the new physicists rightly rejected, they threw out the window the centuries of natural philosophical wisdom accumulated by humanity in all its past.

Then going back to Kuhl's question: Scientific cosmology would be the application of Mathematical Physics to the study of the whole Universe, whereas Philosophical Cosmology would be the Philosophy of Nature, (philosophical physics) as applied to the whole cosmos.

Now this perspective can be extended also to theology, provided again we do not mix, or confuse things while trying to integrate them, that is, without confusing one type of knowledge (or level of knowledge) with another. Maritain was an expert in this task of integrating and seeing the harmony between all the levels of knowledge. The book where he does this, his famous "The Degrees of Knowledge" or *Les Degrés du Savoir* was subtitled: "distinguish to unite." There he describes all the levels and sublevels, going from experimental physics at the lowest, to the highest level of theology and even Mystical knowledge. Doing so, Maritain truly invigorated the whole realm of science and philosophy with a true Christian wisdom and thus purported to "recapitulate all things in Christ."

As a conclusion I'd like to note two things: 1) One related to the four alternatives that Ian Barbour proposes to describe the possible relationships between faith and science, namely: a) conflict; b) independence; c) integration; d) dialog. I would choose *integration* as described before, that is, as a body and soul integration, science providing the data (the physical body so to speak) and philosophy and faith providing the *soul* or interpretation of those otherwise disparate and purely quantitative data. 2) The other point is related to the science and faith *dialog* which was, apparently, the view promoted by our late Pope John Paul II. That dialog, I think, can only be fruitful if the level of philosophy, and specifically, philosophy of nature, is present in the discussion. Suppress philosophy, suppress pure human rationality and you end up with a continual misunderstanding of scientists by theologians and of theologians by scientists. We will be repeating the Galileo drama forever. In conclusion, then, only when a philosophical physics, a philosophy of nature and a philosophical cosmology intervene in the dialog, will we ever harmonize the precise nature of experimental and mathematical science with the highest truths of Sacred Scripture.

**Postiglione:**    I have a letter written to Father Bob Brungs, I want to enter into the proceedings, from Father Walter Ong, SJ., professor of humanities at St Louis University and noted lecturer and author of many books, among them, *Orality and Literacy*. Ong died in 2003 at the age of ninety. I'd like the cosmologists, our speakers and anyone else to respond to his thoughts. Although written in 1984, this letter poses a conviction worth considering and pondering. He wrote:

"…the central intellectual (and emotional) problem in the Church's realization of her mission in the world today is that we have no cosmology. We have had none since the Aristotelian spheres and all that went with them were shown not to be there. The absence of a cosmology affects Christology, Ecclesiology and just about everything else in evangelization, including especially any real planning for the real future. For metaphysics, you need a physics."

**Barr:**   I don't agree with that statement. I think we have a cosmology which modern science gives us. And I don't see anything about it (that modern scientific cosmology) that's incompatible or in tension with or embarrassing to the Church's fundamental teaching. What is missing is not cosmology but a philosophical language that can mediate between the world of scientific thought and the world of theological thought.

Now in the Middle Ages there was this great Aristotelian synthesis, which Ong mentioned in that quote, that provided a common language . The scientists of those days (the natural philosophers) spoke in exactly the same concepts as theologians did. It was all seamlessly integrated in Aristotelian Thomism, but unfortunately that synthesis broke down; and it *had* to break down because that synthesis doesn't work anymore. As a result, it has left us with a void – scientists and theologians speak different languages. And as Francisco Muller noted, the place where they meet is on the ground of philosophy. I don't think there has been developed a philosophical language where they can meet adequately. It's not something that can be solved overnight. Unfortunately! A lot of this work should have been done in the last two or three hundred years and for various reasons it wasn't. And it may take a long time for it to be accomplished.

Actually, I am somewhat of a fan (though not an uncritical admirer) of Bernard Lonergan. I think he took some steps in the right direction. Unfortunately he runs into a lot of opposition from other kinds of Thomists, but that's what I think is missing – the philosophical language.

We see and hear "you scientists are doing good stuff, but basically you are talking only about the measurable quantitative superficial aspects of phenomenon, appearances of things." They continue "If you want to know what things really are in themselves, their essences, you have to leave behind what the sciences tell you and rise to this level of metaphysics." That's not true. Modern physics *does* tell you the essences of things. It doesn't tell you essence of everything, but if you want to know what makes copper, copper, for example, what makes iron, iron, and so on, physics serves well. Why does copper have the properties it has? The nature of something is its essence in so far as it is grounding the properties of things. The properties of things flow from its essence. Why does copper have the properties it has? Why does it conduct electricity? Why does it reflect light this way? And so on. That is what physics tells us. It gives us insight into the nature of copper, and why it's copper and not something else.

So, Philosophers in the church have to start doing some hard work to come to terms with science. They have to understand what science is doing and how it does it. Only then will philosophy, theology and science be able to arrive at a common language. That is the problem, a common language, not the lack of a cosmology.

**Consolmagno:** The heart of the split, going directly to your comment, Dr Barr, is between the "techie world" and the philosophical world. I have a book coming out next month *(God's Mechanics: How Scientists and Engineers Make Sense of Religion*, October, 2007) that talks about the religious life of "techies" — those who work in science and technology – and that could include most of us here at this symposium. We would recognize the type, in fact, there is nothing in the book that you don't already know, as techies. The scary thing is the first time I saw the book I was terrified at how thin a volume it is, because I had put my life's work into it is. But one of the comments I wrote, was recognizing that Jesus was a techie: Jesus was a carpenter. He was someone who worked in the physical world and as a kid wanted to know how things worked, I'm sure.

Imagine a group of philosophers at a meeting like this. All of us techies at the same meeting have our stereotypical evil ideas of those secret philosophers who don't even know how to make the microphones work. Imagine that group of philosophers when Larry, the Cable Guy shows up. Will they give him any respect? That was Jesus, the carpenter, trying to talk to the Scribes and Pharisees. Their problem was that Jesus was a techie. It was not just that he was male and smarter than everyone else. It's that he worked with the physical universe. That being the case, this intolerance goes on in both directions.

You are talking about how the church needs philosophers, Dr. Barr. The techie refrain often is "If only these philosophers would learn a little bit of physics and really know what we are doing, they'd be a whole lot smarter." What really happens to most techies in most churches is that the philosopher and the words of philosophy coming out of the poor guy in the pulpit during his homily, is similar to "Mildred" listening to the pointy-headed boss, in the comic strip Dilbert. And, as a result, you just ignore him. It doesn't really matter what the church philosophers or theologians say about anything because no one is paying attention among the techies. This is actually a bad thing because it does matter what theologians and philosophers say, but this gulf — recalling the analogy of the gulf in the gospel of Luke (16:19-26) between Lazarus and the rich man – that gulf is still there.

I will finish with my comment by taking issue again with something Francisco Muller said. It's wonderful that we are all taking issue with you, Francisco, at least you had something to say – so that makes it a good argument for sure. When you quote Ian Barbour, and Marianne, when you quote the letter from Walter Ong, SJ, I have to say that it's four different ways that science and theology are speaking to each – it's not just "look at the four of them and choose one"; it's that all four of them take place and thank heavens for that. We need conflict between the two because that is the only way that one is going to correct the other. We need times when we can just go off and do our science and our theology. We need times when we are integrated and times when we are just having a pleasant conversation over dinner. True, we don't have a cosmology anymore, and thank heavens for that. Because look how stultifying it was in the Middle Ages when we clung too closely to the cosmology we had.

An interesting thing happened in the Jesuit schools after the Copernican and especially Newtonian revolution. The Church after Galileo demanded, *ordered* that the Copernican cosmology could not be taught in their schools. Any person up for ordination who wanted to learn the cosmology and theology to become a priest, had to learn the Aristotelian "stuff." That held true until the 1750's, and actually the last Jesuit General Congregation before the suppression passed a resolution stating that the Jesuits endorsed Aristotelian physics. Well, nobody paid attention to them either. How often do general congregations really change people's minds? About as often as a syllogism does.

What actually happened was that the Newtonian Physics was taught in the Jesuit Schools but not in the philosophy department anymore. It was taught in the mathematics department. At the same time that the Jesuit philosophers were clinging to the Aristotelian philosophy, the Jesuit mathematicians in the classroom next to them were happily teaching the Copernican system. The map of the Moon made by the Jesuits in 1670 has as its most prominent crater – Copernicus. When they were challenged with that, they said, "Of course, Copernicus' crater is all by itself." "Tycho Brahe is surrounded by all these other craters, oh sure!" So, I'm saying that conflict is sometime a good thing as long as we are not stuck only in conflict or only in polite dialog, only in talking with our own disciplines, and so on. We need all of it.

**Barr:**   Michael Heller's book, *Catholic Physics,* is a PhD dissertation and a very scholarly study of the way science was dealt with in Jesuit colleges in Germany between 1650 and 1750. That was of course a kind of critical period when modern science was emerging. It was a period when the church philosophers should have been coming to grips with the new way of looking at this world and trying to broaden, make more flexible, integrate these ways of thinking. Although they didn't do that, I can't criticize too severely because they had their own immediate problems. There were practical reasons why they tried to stick to the Aristotelianism. But, I felt sad as I read that book because, if they had done more work at that time, we would have less work to do now. – in forging a philosophical language where the two sides can talk to each other – scientists and theologians.

**Sollee:**   I mentioned earlier about Descartes in the 1600s standing up in front of the theological faculty in Paris and telling the theologians bluntly – it is *my* job to talk about God. Somehow or other, theologians and philosophers are bashful about being assertive now that science is seemingly in the lead. Theologians and philosophers alike are trailing behind and trying to catch up.

**Cross:**   I'd like to comment on what I see as a communication impasse. That's why we have ITEST for many years. I've sat here at many conferences trained as a scientist interested in theology and not understanding what theologians were saying. It's really coming home to me now because I agreed to work with Sister Marianne on gathering material for a book on Father Brungs' thoughts and writings. I'm reading his book, *You See Lights Breaking Upon Us,* 1989, a statement of his position about the biomedical revolution and its impact on the church. I'm having an extremely difficult time. I'm now retired and I have time to do this, but I'm finding it very difficult. I spent a long time teaching scientific research methods so I think I know something about it. If I don't I've spread a lot of bad information. Of course in the social sciences, the methods are different from those of the physical sciences. But still, they share many aspects.

My own understanding of my religion and my belief is all based on this theory of knowledge, epistemology, of scientific methodology, the discovery of the truth. When I read Bob Brungs' book, I admire it and it moves me, but I don't understand it. I don't know how he comes up with his conclusions. They just well up from his depths. He sees the union of men and women as the primary symbol of the union of God and humanity. He sees very interesting things, but the methodology I don't understand. I don't know how theologians … one thing I've concluded is that Father Brungs is not a theologian; he's a religious thinker. To continue my thought, theologians do have scientific or quasi-scientific methods for doing the work that they do, but even if that's the case, I don't understand them. If I understood the methodology of theology and the methodology of spirituality or religion which I think is what I'm reading in Brungs' book, then it would solve many of my problems. This is my comment on this communication impasse that I think we are addressing here and now.

**Tucker:** My question is addressed to our panelists and all present in reference to our project, *Exploring the World, Discovering God (EWDG)*. We have to help teachers first and then students to make faith/science connections while respecting the disciplines of science and theology. As a result are we going to be able to raise up a group of people who think about faith and science differently – as complementary? Or is the gulf too wide.

**Abell:** Please take this in the right sense. I agree with Bob Brungs' idea, his dream, and if we are going to make any progress at all in that direction, we have to get them while they are young.

**Consolmagno:** I'm going to use a good chunk of what I had prepared for my final remarks because they fit well here. We have the best example of how the message can be effective in the person of Jesus Christ. He told stories! The message comes across not through philosophical arguments, but through stories. And the stories to tell are the stories of the people who have experienced it – the great scientists of the past and so on. A good example of this was Francisco Muller's presentation on clergy in science during the Saturday afternoon break. That's the story that needs to be told.

Did you come up with the idea of a wall poster --- pictures and one paragraph descriptions of famous clergy scientists through history, Francisco? Because if you go through the Royal Society of London, for example, the main place where science was published in the 17th and 18th centuries, that's where Maxwell's equations were published in 1865. This is where Isaac Newton published a paper on how to make a Newtonian telescope.

Go through and see who was publishing. It was always clergy, until the middle of the 19th century. Members of the clergy were the only people who had the education and the free time to go out and gather leaves and sort and classify them. What is most of the science that we do? It's gathering data, sorting data and putting the info on little 3 by 5 cards, and so on. What do we call that kind of work? It's clerical work. Why is it called clerical work? Because it was done by clerics.

Tell stories! When I was a little kid, my science teachers were Sister Margaret Mary, Sister Coletta Marie and Sister Margaret. And by the way, they were the people who told me there is a Vatican Observatory.

One of the hardest problems I have as a Jesuit speaking about science and religion to the public, and one of the biggest things I have to overcome, is to try to figure out why anyone would think there *is* a God problem? It never occurred to me that there was. And that is the tragedy of the Creationists. They are playing into the myth that there is a conflict between science and religion. They are providing the fodder for the Richard Dawkins's and Daniel Dennett's of the world. And that's the tragedy.

**Barr:**   I want to make a distinction and clarify what I was saying before. I don't think we need to wait around until some new Thomas Aquinas sits down and works out a very sophisticated philosophy with epistemology, metaphysics and so on, before we can do anything. In fact I think some people make a mistake (there are books out there but I won't mention names) trying to bridge the gap between science and religion. They say, "First we'll teach you all of Neo-Thomist philosophy. You can't really understand or relate science or faith until you have five semesters of Neo-Thomism, and then we'll start to talk." That's not necessary.

First the problem is that the history of science has been told with an ideological spin for a couple of hundred years. Just serendipitously historical writers found that there were lots of Catholic priests who made contributions to science and it really blew my mind when I discovered a few years ago that a Jesuit priest, Francesco Grimaldi, discovered the diffraction of light. Diffraction of light is an essential thing in many branches of physics. I studied physics in college and graduate school and no one ever mentioned that diffraction of light was discovered by a priest. Then I found more and more examples and so I began to comb libraries for books in English about priest scientists and contributions of clergy to science. I found one tiny little book published in 1904 with only about five priests included in the volume. Nothing since then has ever been published, but it is a huge story that should be told.

What is the actual history of the Church's involvement in science? This is really dynamite. Let's correct the history instead of endlessly arguing about the Galileo case — which was an exception to a rule (one episode, though a very important one) in an 800 year relationship between the Church and science. The trouble is, the Galileo affair is the *only* thing many people know about the relationship between Church and science. I often ask my audiences to tell me the first thing that comes to mind with the question of the Church and Science. Whose name? Galileo! That's all they've heard. Have they heard of Grimaldi, Lemaitre, and others. Let's tell stories about them.

Another thing is to deal with things at the concrete level. We don't need an elaborate philosophy to respond to questions about extra-terrestrial life, the Big Bang. People sometimes ask me what about quantum creation of universes, and will science some day explain how that could happen? They worry about that. Does that mean that science will explain the Big Bang and we'll have no need for a Creator? That's a concrete question which you can answer by explaining to them what the Church means by "creation." Deal with the concrete questions.

Actually, I'm quite an optimist on this kind of thing. Many people are frightened of science, they don't understand it; there is a math fear. This fear in some leads them to think that every discovery in science will undercut what they believe in faith. They are afraid that tomorrow science will discover something that will force them to abandon some belief. This is where the scientists who are Christian can help. There is nothing to fear because a lot of what science is discovering is helping us. I mention in my book that the trend of discoveries in the last hundred years is actually not pointed more toward materialism and hedonism but actually more toward supporting a fairly traditional theology.

So, things are very hopeful in my opinion and experience. One of the very hopeful things is that we have more scientists who are believers. We have Francis Collins who wrote the book, *The Language of God,* Owen Gingerich who wrote a book, *God's Universe.* It's when we start to tell our story and make our case that the situation will begin to change for the better. It's just that we've been sitting back on our heels and letting the other side dominate the conversation for about 200 years.

**Sollee:** I was in Colorado for 15 years in my observatory, and had many young people and college students come through there looking through the telescope at the "heavens" and digesting all that wonder. Gregorian music played in the background, the type of witness I wanted to provide. I wasn't there to tell them about God, the Creator; I was there to show them through their senses all the wonder. When those kids looked through the telescope, and saw the moons of

130

Jupiter, their response was one of awe "Oh, wow!" That was worth every nickel I invested in that Observatory.

Recently, I was listening to a series of lectures[1] on Science and Religion by Lawrence M. Principe of Johns Hopkins. Principe presents a very balanced history of science and brings up the critical foundational role of the church in science. He names many of the people who have been mentioned this weekend. I'm not trying to make money for The Teaching Company, but this series is historically packed with all the names of wonderful scientists in the past who are not really well known by the public.

**Streeter:** I'd like to go back for a time to John Cross's question and take a stab at talking about what theology is and what its method is. In the past theology was the study of God. It was faith seeking understanding. Anselm gave us that. Thomas completed that definition by saying theology was also understanding seeking faith. So he made it cyclic. Thomas made the faith-understanding concept cyclic. The reason for that is that in the first phase of faith seeking understanding, what is presupposed is faith. In the second phase which is much more typical to our day, we cannot presuppose faith. We are living in a divorced world, in a split Cartesian world. And so, in our day, the second half of that cyclic explanation or descriptive definition, is that many people are begging for somebody to help them believe. So, it's understanding seeking faith.

The discipline of theology is unique in the humanities because it stands like a Colossus of Rhodes. It stands with one leg into data that is revelational. That comes from sacred texts and from the whole rumination, the whole pondering of the ecclesial community, the church, under the influence of the Risen Christ through his Spirit, saying, "All the things I've taught you, I will make known to you. It will come back." So we have an understanding that there is a guidance there into truth. We call it infallibility. It's not that the Oracle has "orcked!" Infallibility within the church is a charism – a breath of fire – by which the church will be moved beyond the foolishness of the stance of Galileo's time. Why did it move? Why didn't it stay entrenched? The same with indefectibility. Anyone can see that the church is laden with sin. How can we then talk about indefectibility or the sinlessness of the church? Because there is a fire at work in its belly, in its heart and that fire is going to move the church to constant purification until, like some purified bride without blemish, it is carried over the threshold by her lover into the heart of God.

1 Lawrence Principe, *Science and Religion*. The Teaching Company (The Great Courses consisting of 12 lectures, 30 minutes each on CDs) 2006.

Theology also has a foot into history and time and into the world. Because theology, if it is worth its salt in this day and age, has to be the study of the sacred of God and God's revelation within history. History includes all of scientific unfolding and everything else. So it stands like a discipline that mediates between religious reality and cultural reality. It mediates between religion and culture. Where does that mediation take place? It doesn't take place four feet off the ground or hanging from a bungee cord. It takes place within human consciousness. That human consciousness, the same human consciousness, deals with all of material data and it deals also with the data of its own consciousness working.

In the past we have dealt with data *objectively*. Today we are being called by consciousness philosophers to consider not only the results of our thought, but the process of our getting to those results. We are being asked to look at another set of data that we have not paid much attention to, and that is our own selves as we come to know. And so, yes, we are returning to epistemology. We are saying, "What is knowing?" Do you have an empirically observable charted set of operations that this consciousness goes through? Are you saying "Well, it just happens"? In other words, what is knowing and what type of empirically observed charted set of cognitional operations can you point to as to what that knowing is? That's pretty scientific.

Also then, metaphysics becomes what you know when you know. Metaphysics will include the physics plus it would also include the psychological because you are watching consciousness and its obstructions. Then we're talking about the transcendent realities. So metaphysics would be what you know when you're doing what you do when you know. This is all going on within what's sitting on your chair. And theology then will be drawing from all the data, both of sense and the data of consciousness and what comes with it. That data will be from revelation and from science. The data is dealt with by the same consciousness. Theology makes sure the faith dimension of that data is included and found working in the midst of culture. Where else would it be?

But there's one piece here – we're talking almost a likeness, as John Cross pointed out, to scientific method because we gather the data, ask the questions, come to a judgment. But there's another movement that nobody wants to talk about and that's what Marcianne Kappes pointed out the other day. What do you do when you are grasped by God? What do you do when you look at the statue of Teresa of Avila? This is not somebody's private stuff; this happens to people and it needs to be accounted for. It's called religious experience. It's not something *you* control anymore than you control falling in love. Because when you are grasped by God, when you have religious experience, you're transfixed and you are suddenly in a different state than you were before you had that experience. Just as you are now in love with this lovely lady, or this handsome gentleman, and you were not yesterday — so, you are in a different state. When you are grasped by love, something happens to your cognition.

The grasping by religious love which is very similar to erotic love, means that you are become obsessed with God; you are in love with God. You are in a *state* of being in love with God. This is called grace – two-way grace: One way grace is always present from God's side. But we may not be in love. We are busy about frying fish. If God is now in my horizon, then my horizon today is different from yesterday's horizon. Then my questions come from the inside, from the heart, the depth of that affective religious love. With this grasping my cognition now works within the context of being religiously in love.

This is where Bob Brungs is coming from. Bob is a man in love. When you're not in love if you read somebody else's mail you may make fun of it because you are not in love. And that is what is happening with our friends, the Atheists, our brothers and sisters who are not in love. I look at my brother who married a certain woman and I think, dear God in Heaven, what did he see in her? I'm not in love with her. He sees her differently because of his love. Religiously this is what we call faith. We see from Wisdom, from love's way of seeing. Once grasped by love, we see through that love in faith; with wisdom as its high peak of development.

And then we begin to do our same little dance: gather the data, ask the questions, reach the judgment. We're still going to do that. It's not a different conscious-ness. But it is a consciousness that has moved into that grasping of religious experience. And then we do our little dance, our little *cognitive* dance. That's what I meant about interpenetration, that's what I meant about oiling — they are not separate; the person who is religiously grasped and your scientific thinking. But you will respond because something has grasped your heart. That grasping forms the context in which you do all of your science or all of your psychology, history, or whatever. It is going back to the Ancient Patristic understanding of "theologie" which means that spiritual experience which is the root of all the theological work in the early church. These doctors of the church, Gregory of Nyssa, Ambrose, Augustine, were people in love. They were not doing theology from the neck up. They were doing theology from the heart out and that included the cognitive operations of the human mind.

**McNamara:**   Bob Brungs often used to say that the theology he was interested in was the theology done on your knees. That is a summary of what Sister Carla Mae just said.

**Powell:**   I very strongly agree with Guy in that you don't win any converts to understanding science and religion through philosophical arguments. It is through stories! More important than the stories are seeing the people. We need to find a way to get the scientists to show up in church and not leave the science at the door of the church. They have to talk about their science once they get into the congregation. Steve Kuhl mentioned that there wasn't much history of some of these stories of the people who contributed to science in the past. I just did a Google search here and Wikipedia has a list that is 102 long -- 102 people. Some other source I haven't gotten on to yet has a library of 600 people -- Christians. The Wikipedia web site is List of Christian Thinkers in Science.

We need to change our vantage point from books to the Internet. (laughter) If you have anything to publish yourself, the means are available on the Internet. We need to add to it and make that information available. It amazes me how much the Creationists have put on various web sites compared to what I see among various Christian Churches and their web sites, one of which I partially edit. But we have nothing close to what's available out there. I just toured the Creation Museum and their big emphasis is "Why Genesis Matters." To their understanding, if you don't have a literal belief in the first eleven chapters of Genesis, you lack the cosmology necessary to support all the rest of Christian doctrine. So when we talk about needing a cosmology, I think, yes, we may need one to help complete and support these other doctrines, but in the long run I think we need simply to make science present within the church.

**Pouch:**   I'd like to thank Kevin Powell for ending on the topic of making science present within the Church, because, in fact, that is one of the things I think we need to do with the faith/science apostolate. I'd like to thank Brother Guy for pointing out that conflict, independence, dialogue and integration (Ian Barbour's four models) might all occur between science and religion, and would even amplify this by pointing out that all four probably occur simultaneously, since science is large and involves many people doing many things, and religion is large and involves many people doing many things, and, not surprisingly, the interaction of two complex objects is complex indeed.

I'd like to discuss a number of our techniques for teaching about the relationship of science and faith, not so much to people who are firmly entrenched in one camp or another, but to those, often young, who haven't formed a steadfast view yet and might easily be led astray.

Even though they are true, we don't persuade by presenting historical arguments about the Galileo incident: how Galileo was not tortured, and that Galileo was treated gently compared to what might have happened to someone who did a lot of the stuff that he did in Renaissance Italy (worse things could happen to you than what Galileo endured: they didn't burn him or anything.) It's true, but that argument runs counter to what they've been taught since childhood and is often dismissed as historical revisionism trying to cover our tracks. What is persuasive, what does convince people that science and religion are not in opposition, is actions: actions speak louder than words.

Even though true, we will not persuade by pointing out how many clergy have done science over the years; it is simply dismissed with a claim that if you were educated, you were clergy so it's not really relevant (i.e., they weren't *really* clergy, only educated), nor is it wise to represent the Church as just the clergy, since the clergy are rather a small portion of the Faithful. Nor will we persuade by pointing out that there have been or are lots of Catholics who happen to be scientists and remain Catholic. From my own experience, this is dismissed with the comment that they were just raised Catholic and they never really drifted off. (That last part is usually phrased more hurtfully, but you get the gist.) It is fairly easy for doubters to write off historical arguments about faith-filled scientists as simply the product of their time or circumstances. We don't seem to persuade by showing that science education in Catholic institutions is done well: this is viewed as simply part of having educational institutions.

What does get us taken seriously — and what gets us a lot more credit than we give ourselves credit for — is that we have hospitals. The existence of Catholic hospitals means people take the Church seriously when we talk about health care. Part of this is that we can simply pick up our ball and our bat and go home. (i.e., our not cooperating could be problematic). The Catholic church, and some other churches as well, get taken very seriously on issues relating to health, not because we have a really strong persuasive argument about life-ethics and how this fits into our metaphysics, but because we take it seriously. We take it seriously enough to build hospitals and medical schools. We take it seriously enough to become doctors and nurses and medics. We take it seriously enough to *do* it, not just talk about it or against it.

We need to branch out even further from this, so that when people are thinking of issues of science, and they don't even think "warfare" between science and faith makes sense, anymore than they would think that there is "warfare" between science and driving a car or cooking. No one really worries about how science relates to cooking (OK, biochemists worry about this, and I suppose food engineers and agricultural engineers). We need to reach the point where people look as baffled and ask "Why would you think that Christian faith and science are contradictory?" as they would if they were told that plumbing and yellow are contradictory.

People won't often come to a correct understanding that faith and science are not enemies by deciding that they want to find out about "science's relationship to Catholic thinking" or "Catholic teaching on science" and conducting an internet search or seeking out a book and believing what they find; rather, it will happen as, when they are looking for information on black holes or meteorites, they find good material at the Vatican Observatory. The Vatican (Astronomical) Observatory is a good start. Fr. McNamara's work at the Manila Observatory in the Philippines is another good example of what we need: science done as part of our faith.

We need more examples that illustrate through action how science can serve faith, and how faith motivates much science, and how sometimes they're as independent as faith and plumbing. We need to emphasize that being a scientist can be a *way to put our faith into action*, that one correct way to integrate science and faith is to let Faith dictate the goals. It would help tremendously if the Church had more scientific institutions like a geological survey, an agricultural research service, an agricultural extension service, a public health service, a weather service, and so on, both "pure" and applied, as well as the ordinary faithful *doing* science as an expression of their faith, like agricultural research to feed the hungry, and geological exploration for groundwater to give water to those who thirst; or studying how planets form – to give greater glory to God.

The way for the Church to get out of this non-sense — about religion and science being locked in conflict, or science being the triumph of reason over superstition and religion, or religion being something that people who aren't smart enough to be Communists or other materialists believe in — isn't going to be by philosophical discourse, which puts many people off. It will be done by the faithful actually *being* out in the fields of science and engineering, by being *seen* out *working* in those fields. We teach better by doing than we do by talking. I think it was St Francis of Assisi who said "Preach the Gospel always; use words only if necessary."

**Sheahen:**   At this point we are going to deviate a little bit from what is on the printed schedule. We are going to begin our summaries and observations and reflections by our essayists. We will start with Stephen Barr and then we're going to have a brief break. But we will return for the final Session later in the morning.

**Barr:**   I haven't prepared a formal summary so I'm going to address a few questions. I guess the big question for average people, either in the back or the front of their minds, is the conflict between science and religion. Some people have a pessimistic view. John Polkinghorne has a classification of different scientists and theologians. For example, he refers to Arthur Peacocke as an example of a "revisionist" school; whereas Polkinghorne refers to himself as a "developmental" school. He says that some people think that in order to come to terms with the scientific view of the world, radical revisions of basic Christian doctrines are necessary. That's what the revisionists like Peacocke hold.

Whereas, Polkinghorne contends that no radical revision of doctrine is necessary. I am with him on that. I don't believe that any radical revision of Christian doctrine is necessary. In fact I have a fairly optimistic view about going forward now with dialogue, discussion with science and religion.

I think there are several different levels on this. On the one hand there is what Michael Heller said: I can't remember the exact word that English people have for this, but it is a word that distinguishes between actual Christian doctrine (that which we are committed to believe as Christians, as Catholics) and the world picture or image. People in every age try to integrate their religious beliefs and their other beliefs to give themselves some coherent picture of the world. This involves a kind of imaginative extrapolation from the doctrines. That's inevitable and it shouldn't be stopped. People need that; they have to have some image in mind of how things fit together.

We ran into trouble when people, using the Aristotelian synthesis, got doctrine too closely attached to certain pictures of the cosmos — not coming from the Bible or Christian tradition but from Aristotle and Ptolemy. So you have to avoid getting too attached to these world pictures.

Let's take one example: in the old days people naturally wondered, "Where is Hell? If it's a place, if some people go there, then it's got to be somewhere." So it was quite natural for people in earlier times to figure that Hell is in the bowels of the Earth. Volcanoes and fire come up and you know that there's a lake where fire is erupting. That was part of their imaginative picture — that Hell is somewhere down in the center of the earth. St. Augustine talks about what level of the atmosphere the angels lived in. We are tempted to smile at some of these things. But that was inevitable in those days, and we still do that in our day. We have to have pictures.

What the theologians have to do (in terms of communicating with ordinary people) is to continuously work to purify or distinguish what is "in fact," doctrine and what is imaginative extrapolation. Be very careful of that. That's one issue and that's where a lot of the conflicts come from – the failure to make that distinction. That's the level of actual doctrine. Questions arising from science that can demonstrate that there *is* a conflict with doctrine, then those doctrines have to be radically revised.

For example, the whole question of extra-terrestrial life: It does raise some interesting questions – about Original Sin, about "how does Redemption work if there are ET beings? "Would there be another Incarnation?" and so on. These are really interesting doctrinal questions. Scientists who have studied the Big Bang. How do we square that with our doctrine of Creation? Is the Big Bang the same thing as "The Creation"? Important questions will arise and must be dealt with.

Here is one reason I'm optimistic: consider biological advances today. How does the story of Adam and Eve square with what science is telling us about human origins? I'm fairly optimistic here because there is a very deep Catholic doctrinal, theological and philosophical position which I think has adequate resources for answering most of these questions. For instance I very much like brother Guy's way of looking at the whole question and doctrine of the Incarnation.

Some people, even some theologians I won't name here, have inadequate ideas about what the Incarnation involved. There are actually some well-known people who think that in the Incarnation, God kind of left Heaven (at least the Second Person of the Trinity did, they say) and kind of turned into a man. Meanwhile others think of the Incarnation as a kind of the making of a centaur – half God and half man. If you think of things inadequately like that, there will be problems. If you have the Incarnation on other planets, then what happens? If God left Heaven and came here, he can't simultaneously be on any other planet. So, is God constantly popping in and out of Heaven, or is he half man, half God — a tiny part human, a tiny part octopus, a tiny part Klingon, for instance.

But a lot of the work that was done in the early councils of the church comes to our aid here. We recognize that the Divine Nature underwent no change, and there is a Divine and Human Nature. The Divine Nature is not changed but assumes a human nature without affecting the Divine Nature. So the traditional Catholic doctrinal theological framework, (because it is profound, sophisticated) can handle a question like that.

The same thing applies to the question of the Big Bang and Creation. We don't think of creation as a physical event where some guy took a pool stick, hit a ball and set the ball rolling. Creation isn't just one physical event in a sequence. It's the bringing into being, it's the *giving being* to the whole of created reality in one eternal act. If one understands what creation meant to Augustine and Thomas Aquinas then we recognize that these ideas of creation (theories of how the Big Bang happened, physics theories of what went on in the Big Bang) are simply not a threat at all. Again, one has to bring to these questions, the richness and depth of the Catholic theological, philosophical tradition. And that requires work. As I said, we are in a fairly good position here because our theology is adequate to deal with most of the questions. There are questions which are kind of thorny and puzzling. But I think for a lot of the questions (which many people imagine require a radical revision of doctrine), we are in a position to deal with them quite effectively.

My third point is this: It's not just a question of "Where are the challenges, dangers, threats from science and what are going to do with them?" Science doesn't just throw out challenges and threats; many of the things science is doing are really aids to our faith and religion. Just look at the pictures of the universe that Neyle Sollee and Guy Consolmagno showed us. The heavens tell the glory the God! We see that in so many ways that we never would see without science and technology – the Hubble telescope, the close-ups of the moon and the planets. They are so powerful in showing people the glory of the Heavens — it tells us what the psalmist means when he sings, "the Heaven proclaim the glory of God." So there is a lot that science can help us with, coming to our aid.

In my talk I quoted Minucius Felix: the classic argument of the orderliness of the universe pointing to a Law Giver. Now in the 21st century in fundamental physics we see so much more clearly, deeply the laws of nature. What astonishing, intricate, subtle, deep, profound mathematical structures! The world has an orderliness that goes far beyond what people of ancient times were able to see. They saw regularities in the Heavens; we see so much more now when we deal with theories of physics.

Super String Theory (SST) has now been around for 23 years; the Super String revolution began in 1984. This theory is so mathematically abstract that after 23 years of a very large number of brilliant math physicists working on it, they still haven't come to grips with it. They still don't feel that they understand the mathematics of SST. It's that deep. If that is so, doesn't that point to the fact that there is a Mind, an awesome intellect that conceived such a marvel?

In many ways science can come to our aid provisionally. Some old problems have fallen by the wayside. Here is an example that used to be a very big worry for Christians: the laws of physics were thought to be deterministic (until the 20th century); so how could there be free will if everything was physically determined? Quantum Mechanics advanced beyond Classical mechanics and eliminated this question by showing the laws are *not* deterministic.

# Astronomy/Cosmology Breakthroughs and the God Question

## Session 5

*Proceedings of the ITEST Symposium - September, 2007*

**Sollee:** The famous evolutionary biologist, Ernst Meyer, said that virtually all biologists are religious in the deepest sense of the word, even though it may be a religion without revelation. The Unknown and then maybe the Unknowable still evokes a sense of humility and awe. For myself, as one who deals with disease and health, as well as for the ordinary person in the "pews," I think that science can give us a sense of mystery, awe and wonder. And as Mayer says, "humility." This seems to me an important characteristic lacking in many quarters today: a sense of humility.

To the ordinary person, scientists can be perceived as pompous and egotistical (*aka scientific imperialism*). This may reflect CP Snow's Two Cultures, the literary and the scientific. I have tried to bridge these two cultures. Being a physician and an "educated outsider" in physics and astronomy, I see myself as a bridge between the layperson and the scientist. I would want to be a person who reflects the wonder and mystery of all creation.

One of the things I tried to bring out in my talk was the physical and spiritual evolution of the human person. Consciousness with its biological complexity has arisen out of stardust, so that for the Christian, matter matters. For the Christian "all that came to be had life in Christ"; and that matter has consciousness (in some sense inchoate) in it from the beginning; and that the fire in the equations of physics (Steven Hawkins) reflects, somehow the divine "energies" of the Creator. Eastern Christians would say that it is natural to be supernatural. Another way to think of "string theory" is that God has each of us tethered on our special "string" being drawn back to our original Source.

As people become more and more conscious of this indwelling Presence, they will become more fully human and fully alive. Karl Rahner then will have been vindicated for his statement that the Christian of the future will be a mystic or not at all. So we are all mystics in training, so to speak. Thomas Merton said that if we don't have a contemplative orientation to our lives, then we certainly will not find our true self and real happiness.

So in summary, the "God Question" being at the tail end of the physics and astronomy topics, seems to capture the orderly sequence in the evolving growth and development (emergence) of physical and spiritual knowledge. One could even say the growth and development of the spiritual organism. I would hope and pray that the beauty of mathematics, physics and astronomy would arouse in us wonder and mystery so that we could "taste and see" the Source of all Wisdom.

**Consolmagno:**   I want to go back to the title and the topic, Astronomy Break-throughs and the God Question. Astronomy is wonderful because anyone with a pair of eyes can go outside at night and see the stars. That's something that I have to share that Stephen doesn't get to share and that was pointed out very clearly. When I was in the Peace Corps I was able to take my little telescope up-country and point it at Jupiter and share the image of Jupiter with the men and women in the village. They had exactly the same reaction as the people in Cambridge Massachusetts had as they viewed the planet from the top of the roof of the Harvard college observatory. Astronomy is wonderful because it reminds us that the universe is bigger than us. The universe is not flat and round with a dome over it with "me" at the center. The universe is bigger than that and astronomy reminds us of that.

Astronomy kept me from being horribly homesick when I was in Kenya. I remember asking myself when I was in the Peace Corps why I was wasting my time doing astronomy when people are starving in the world? And I discovered much to my surprise that people are starving for astronomy too. Astronomy is one of the things that dogs and cats don't do. Only human beings do astronomy. To deny someone astronomy because they are from the Third World, is to deny them their humanity. I think you can see the connection between astronomy and religion. All of those things I just mentioned are also true of religion. And it's not an accident that when the Vatican decided to open an Institute, it was an Observatory. Historical reasons went into it, but it also felt right.

Astronomy breakthroughs is part of our topic this weekend. All three of us agreed that the word "breakthroughs" was a wonderful choice of words. A breakthrough is different from a revolution. We are not overturning the past. We are standing on top of the past and bursting through the ceiling *or* bursting through the basement as Stephen Barr mentioned – trying to find the deepest foundations. But the word "breakthrough" carries the implication of change, of correction, of humility, humiliation, recognizing that what I thought I understood, I don't. I found that what I thought I had all worked out, had much more to it than I realized. And that is very unsettling. One of the hardest things about being a teacher — most of us in this room have been teachers – is having tell your student, "No, you're wrong; go back and do it again." And I think the only thing harder is being the student who has to hear it.

But that is one of the joys of science – that we are told by the universe (our teacher) when the experiment doesn't turn out the way we expected, "No, you're wrong, go back and do it again." We can argue with the Pope if he says we're wrong; we can argue with our professors if they tell us we're wrong; we can argue with Mom when she says we're wrong, but we can't argue with Mother Nature. So in a sense it's more unsettling to deal with it, but in another sense it's also easier because we know that the authority of the experiment is absolute.

There is a wonderful story about Albert Einstein. He was confronted with a fair amount of evidence in the 1920s that disproved the theory of general relativity. He said, "Oh the experiment has got it wrong." They said, "How can you say that?" Einstein replied, "I know the theory is right" — and then he uttered that famous phrase, "God is subtle; He is not malicious." Abraham Pais's biography, entitled, *Subtle is the Lord: The Science and the Life of Albert Einstein* (1982), plays on those words of Einstein. In other words Einstein is saying, "My theory is so good that God wouldn't have done this to me." And in that case, Einstein was right; the experiments had gone wrong. As a humorous aside there's another story going around about Hans Kung, that he could never become Pope because then he would no longer be infallible. (Laughter)

The humility that comes from being a scientist should be operative when science challenges our theology. It would be really easy to be a theologian who talks only to other theologians who agree with him because people who disagree with us are obviously wrong. To be a philosopher who talks only to other philosophers who agree with him obviously becomes like those other philosophers who don't know what is important. But you can't get away with that when you're doing science. This brings me to the wonderful phrase of Pope John Paul II in his famous letter in 1988 to George Coyne, SJ, on the nature of science and religion

"Science can purify religion from error and superstition; religion can purify science from idolatry and false absolutes. Each can draw the other into a wider world, a world in which both can flourish."

So much of what we do as human beings is superstition. Superstition is doing the same thing over and over again in the hope that you get the same result even if we can't see a causal connection between the two. For example, the baseball player who hits a home run thinking it was because he wore a certain color socks, says to himself, "If I wear them again tomorrow without washing them, I'll hit another home run." That's silly and it's superstition; yet it's a very human thing to do. We do it in our science when we talk about the repeatability of experiments. That's how science progresses. If I flip the switch and the light goes off, and I do it again and the light goes off, and a third time the same thing happens, I'm going to presume from now on that the switch is what controls the light. How do

I know it's not just a long series of coincidences? And yet in science we assume that a sufficiently long string of coincidences gives a scientific law. And that's not always true. Sometimes it really *is* a long string of coincidences. But new arguments, new experiments allow us eventually to stumble upon that truth and back off and say, "Ok what I thought was a scientific law isn't what I thought it was. The light is still there; the switch is still there; the truth is still out there, but the way in which I draw the connections has to be done more deeply." We have to be brave enough to do that in our theology as well.

A faith that is afraid of science has no faith. A faith that is afraid has no faith. It's one thing to say, "Let's all be brave." But it's a whole other thing to actually *be* brave.

There's astronomy and there's the breakthrough. What's the God question? I really was taken aback by Steve Kuhl's response and commentary yesterday because he got to me. He leveled an accusation at me that was square on. And I don't like being told that I'm insufficient. He pointed out that I never addressed what I thought the God question was. Then he made some suggestions as to what the God question might be. Is it an existence question? Is it the meaning of salvation question? he asked. And I'm thinking, "I don't know; that's not my question." But of course I never told him what my question was in my paper, so it's my own fault. What is the God question?

The God question! Given the fact that there is a God – which I believe for a whole string of other reasons connected with my own history and my own faith – what does astronomy tell me about that God? And how do I, as an astronomer, go about making that connection? As an astronomer, I make assumptions, and then I see if they are consistent with my observations and if they are, then I won't throw them away — which is not the same thing as believing them As long as my assumptions are not inconsistent with the observations, I still hold them as hypotheses, as possibilities. But when I see an assumption that isn't going to work, then I say "Fine, then I don't pursue that."

What do I mean by, "What does astronomy tell me about the God question?" In astronomy I'm seeing God the Creator who has been associated traditionally with God the Father. Who is the God that I actually know in my faith? Then, I say, "it's God the Son because I read about him in a book." Or... "it's God the Holy Spirit because that's been my experience." No, it's God! You can't split him up and divide him that way.

And yet there certainly is in Scripture, in Jesus, that we have a person with a personality that is very accessible to us, and that is the personality that I can compare with the personality of the Creator. What do I see in the personality of the Creator who made creation? I can tell you a lot about Shakespeare by the plays that he wrote. If Shakespeare had written a play with a character named Bill Shakespeare wandering around spouting off opinions, I could say, "Oh, you see, that's how I learned about the author." That's what we do in literature. We ask who is the Point of View character, the one reflecting the opinions of the author? What do I see in Creation, in Astronomy. First of all beauty. Beauty is big to this God. Beauty is not something that happens by accident. Beauty is something that is there by design. I see phenomenal complexity that arises out of very simple principles and I say, "Ah, now I know what JS Bach was doing." That's a game that this Creator must play.

And I see stories. I can see from the cloud in Orion where stars are being formed to the planetary nebulae at the death of the stars with gas clouds bursting off and the gas and dust from those clouds then becoming more clouds, and more stars are being born. I see stories, I see beginning, middle, end. I see an evolution in the stars.

There are other different ways in which God could have created the universe. This is the way that God chose to create: through principles that involve change and relationship. That is a word that I wouldn't have thought to connect until listening to you all here this weekend. But relationship is built into all of us. Yet, "you need a supernova over there to get to the planet there, and so on." And you say, "Yes, that is relationship." Stars don't just occur in a vacuum. These are the connections I can make to the personality of the Incarnate representative whom I can read about in my book: a God who loved to tell stories; a God who is big into relationships; a God who loved beauty and wept at ugliness.

When we take these lessons and try to present them to people outside this room, how do we do it? I've already mentioned story telling. I'm going to mention one other twist. We talked about arguments as if they were truths. Science doesn't deal with truths — and I've said that a few times already. What we use these arguments for, what we use illustrations for, is not to prove a point, but to teach a point, to illustrate the point we are trying to make. I love the argument that states that the Bible must be read literally and not as poetry. It creates a false dichotomy. Science is poetry. The falling of my pen follows a path that is like the solution of the equation of Newton's gravity. "Like," as my English teacher would tell me is evidence of a simile. The laws of physics are metaphors for what is happening in the physical . They *aren't* the physical . We can only speak in metaphor; we can only speak in poetry, especially when we are speaking about love and the things we are in love with – whether it's God or astronomy. When I meet my beloved I don't say, "Gee, my pulse has gone up 2.3 percent." It doesn't work! So let's go forth and do some poetry. Thanks for having me here.

**Kuhl:**   First of all I want to thank our three major speakers for really doing a marvelous job of leading us into a very complex conversation about things that touch all aspects of life. For my comments, I echo strongly what our three essayists said, but I want to focus on the initial paper too and ask how often do we look at the questions I addressed to them. Of course Guy just pointed out his reaction and response to those questions.

But that part of the title of this symposium: "The God question" to me was very important and I came here thinking, partly from the popular media presentation of the way things happen as well as from your papers, that it seemed the way that cosmology and astronomy engaged theology was by proving theology's object for people so that they could have some reason to begin to be interested in theology. Of course, my objection was that we don't have a God exactly as an object. God is not an object the way the creation is an object, and so this is a category mistake to think in those terms. The essayists and participants addressed my objection during the discussion that occurred here this weekend.

What I did learn was how emphatic Guy and scientists are in saying that they don't really prove anything. I'm not sure I'm convinced of that. I think you prove a lot of things. The question of whether or not people want to believe it is another question about what scientists sometimes prove. Because of our fallen nature we want to hang on to *us* as the center and as the orbit around which everything rotates, including the way in which we adjudicate knowledge and proofs. That is a part of the fallen nature of humanity. We are threatened when events or people question and upset our stable orbit, as we understand it. But I understand from Newtonian physics to the modern quantum theories, that this world is not the nice, neat, mechanical system that the Deists and others try to use to assert their positions.

Asking the question about God: I think astronomy is very humble in terms of what it can say about God; and Guy, I applaud both your commitment as a Christian in science to your Lord and Creator and to this Lord's Creation and your enthusiasm for being a steward of it. Actually the role of humility comes in greatly in understanding our stewardship. And being a steward applies to humanity as a whole and to each individual who has a part and role to play in the ongoing holistic stewardship of this world. An important part of that stewardship is knowing more about this world so that we can deal with it and interact with this Creation with integrity. If I understand anything about the image of God or the *Imago Dei* described in the Genesis story, it's not giving us some philosophical principle about human beings. Rather, it is saying we are created in the image of God. We are God's stewards and our call is not to prove God's existence, but rather to take care of what God has created. We can't help but do that without bearing witness to that God at least as believing Christians. So there is a sense in which we always bring our faith into our stewardship, and in this case into the science of cosmology, astronomy and other sciences.

One other thing I learned this weekend, was that I appreciated that little book on Catholic scientists and science. One of my concerns was how Christians today would use Thomas Aquinas. I suggested in my paper that even Protestants are increasingly looking to Aquinas for certain things. The question is what should we look to him for in this modern world view? I suggested that modern Thomistic studies are telling us, not to look at Thomas the philosopher; rather, look at Thomas, the Biblical Christian theologian. And I think that's what I was hearing in this room this weekend. Maybe, we as church people, stake too much hope and confidence in former philosophical and cosmological ideas that have served to explain our faith, rather than using, say, a new scientific discovery – as we learn more about that – to further explain it, to help us express our faith.

One concept that I raised before didn't get a lot of attention. I'm referring to that part of the Christian Confession about God, and it comes straight from the lips of Jesus himself. Moreover, it is at the heart of the meaning of his soteriological mission. It is not only a God who is this wonderful awesome, marvelous Creator of the world that Christians confess, but a God who finally holds us accountable for what we do in this world. I described that taking it from St Paul and Jesus Himself: there is something called "The Wrath of God" that is revealed also in this world, this cosmos, this creation. So, part of the problem we have as Christian theologians and as Christian people, is to admit that we do have a God who wants to hold us accountable. The question then is: Does that find a place in understanding ourselves, as human beings, to entertain that thought? In other words in the Christian tradition, repentance becomes an essential part of our Christian vocation.

The Gospel says to repent and believe the Good News of the forgiveness of sins. It doesn't avoid God's word of judgment. The primary image in the Scriptures is not so much God the Artificer, the one who makes this great building of the cosmos, but the God who is the King who rules over it and makes judgments about it. As I described the soteriological question, it presupposes that aspect of God as well. That's why I pressed Guy Consolmagno on that point: for example, where do you see sin? Where do you see the judgment of God in astrophysics? Where do you find it? I wasn't surprise that my questions caused some consternation. Biblically we find it in the stewards who were not practicing good stewardship — the stewards who were not willing to be faithful to their calling. But that does affect the world and our own stewardship tremendously. It probably has ramifications for the fall, all the way back to whatever the cosmological constants might be. But certainly within the Christian tradition, the soteriological element of the stewards of creation, makes all the difference in the world for the cosmos as a whole. I'm not sure that's a scientific question or whether it can be answered in that mode. But it's certainly an important question that needs to be addressed when theology and science engage one another.

Finally, I want to comment on the anthropic principle in relation to this. Using a quote from my opening paper: "…[anthropic principle] the idea that the universe is the logical outworking of some inner purpose or telos, whether mystical or naturalistic, designed to bring forth intelligent human life. We, the human creatures, are the ultimate explanation of the cosmos." In other words the universe is so finely tuned that we just have to be the reason for it. I disagree with that, for I see latent in that kind of approach to the anthropic principle, Original Sin, that is to say, *we* are at the center and *we* are the reason and that everything exists for us indeed. I don't want to deny, at the same time, the central role that humanity has to play in the creation, and it certainly does. The important thing is how does the anthropic principle point to our being faithful stewards. We are the image of God. To be faithful stewards, we as Christians think that we need to be redeemed from this thing called Sin, from this thing called "The Fall," from this myopic outlook that is all too prevalent. It will affect our science, this vision of us in this world. Given the anthropic principle, we do have a central role to play but it is one of great humility, of responsible stewardship and service in the midst of all this.

Thus, in the Christian world view the human being always looks in two directions: 1) towards the Lord who is the Creator yet is *other than* the creation, the One to whom we are accountable, and 2) to the creation which is the responsibility that the Lord has laid upon us. But the two directions always fit together even though they are distinct. I'll use an example: the worker is accountable both *to* the boss and *for* the product going to the customer even though they are distinct.

The Christian world view linked with responsible stewardship is a very helpful concept for us to understand, especially when science and theology engage each other.

**Mahfood:**   I also have to rethink my whole cosmology. We have a professor at Kenrick Seminary, Fr. Michael Witt, who has put together more than one hundred hours of audio on Church history, medieval and modern and posted it on his web site. This summer I downloaded 75 hours of the talk to a little device the size of a quarter and carried it around with me. Any time I was driving or walking from my office to the cafeteria. I was able to listen to it and completed about 40 hours of Church history in this way. One of the things that struck me was his talk about evangelizing China. In this section he began with priests training the Chinese to be medical doctors. By doing that, by teaching the people practical skills, these priests were engaged in something he called "pre-evangelization." Once the Chinese understood the science, they then said, "Well, we now have the formal and the material cause, now what is the efficient cause?" They moved from learning about science into asking, "From whence does this science come?" And ultimately the final cause, "To where does this science lead us?" The priests were able then to evangelize further in that direction.

This reminds me of Neyle Sollee's work in the Observatory or where Guy Consolmagno works in his Vatican Observatory. Young people are coming and looking and contemplating the planets. They are experiencing these things through their senses first and then asking questions about the implications later.

It would seem that in studying natural philosophy, with how things work, we build a foundation for our effort to understand creation. Our friend, Aristotle, begins his Metaphysics with that tack. He said that all men desire to know and this is evidenced by the delight they take in their senses. (We'd apply his meaning in the present day to 'all women,' too, of course). So, it is through our senses that we come to know God, and we are called to taste and see, but we are also told that the ear has not heard nor the eye seen the glory that God has in store for us.

When engaging our senses, we have to allow a process through which our senses lead us to philosophical reflection and through such reflection to an articulation of theological faith. I think that's where Descartes took a wrong turn when he said we can't trust our senses at all because our senses are deceiving. Our senses are our first tools. While it might seem easy to dismiss them in favor of an intellect that can sustain itself, an intellect that *is* because it *thinks*, we cannot lose sight of the fact that the intellect needs a substance *about which* to think. This substance is something that we as incarnational beings have to grasp materially before we can process it immaterially. This is, perhaps, the relationship between the body and the soul, for the soul is the form of the body.

So this is where we start – with our senses that give us the phantasms we need to guide our reason, which enables us to move to faith. I think then that we ought to be able to see a relationship between those things: the senses, reason and faith. I think there is a practical application of all this, and what theology might do is "pre-evangelize" through following the technical vocation of Christ. As Brother Guy mentioned earlier, by showing people how they might use their senses as natural tools and showing how we might move in the direction of our ability to reason based on what it is we have accomplished through our natural tools, we might then move from the natural to the supernatural along that kind of path.

That is sort of where I am in my progress from what our discussions have been. I'm not entirely certain how that plays out systematically. I hope the theologians who know more than I can take it from there.

**Pouch:** Can I point out that they've tried to prove to you that scientists don't prove anything? And that therefore they have succeeded in proving that they don't prove anything?

**Mahfood:** Well, it's not a question of proving, after all, but, in the words of Dominican William Wallace, of coming to a truth that is clearer and more complete than the truths we already possess.

**Postiglione:** Before Tom Sheahen closes the meeting as the facilitator and Vice Director of ITEST, I would like to add my comments as acting director of ITEST. As we were talking this morning, all I could think of was the request, almost a plea, that Bob Brungs challenged us with at the ending of the 2005 conference on *Biotechnology, Law and Theology*. He asked, "Where are the Psalmists of the 21st century? Who in the scientific community sings of the beauty of Creation today, from the beauty of the universe, the comets, the planets, -- where are they? Why don't scientists look at what they are doing, and sing of the beauty of God?" he concluded. I think we have our answer this weekend. We definitely do have 21st century Psalmists right here in this room, and I thank especially the presenters and all the participants who sang gloriously of God's wonder and beauty.

**Sheahen:** As we come to the end of the conference, the question for all of us is: what do we take home? That's one of the catch phrases in contemporary management theory – the take home part of the meeting. It is really for each individual to reflect on the things you've heard and think about what all of this means – the God question: is it a question of God's existence or is it a question of what we are supposed to do about it? And I think as Christians we generally jump to the second one. To a great extent that is probably what we could be thinking about on our way home.

I cannot constructively add appreciably to what our essayists have just summarized for us. I think it has been a wonderful symposium and I thank all of you for your participation and hope we will see you again next year. But in particular in the time ahead, take these ideas you formulated this weekend with you and start speaking out and being one of the people who sing the glory of God. Thank you all for coming.

**Postiglione:** And thanks, Tom, for a marvelous job.

*Our main speakers l to r: G. Consolmagno, N. Sollee, S. Barr*

*l to r: K. Powell, Fr. McNamara, SJ, Carla Mae Streeter, OP*

# Astronomy/Cosmology Breakthroughs and the God Question

Appendix

*Proceedings of the ITEST Symposium - September, 2007*

*We received the following letters from two of the seminarians who attended the symposium. Studying at Kenrick-Glennon Seminary in St Louis, Missouri, Vince White and Kevin Vogel show that they not only grasped the essence of the symposium but were also able to apply some of the principles to their life of faith and their academic studies.*

I attended the ITEST conference mainly because of the topic. I am keenly interested in astronomy and cosmology. This interest started when I was doing my undergraduate work. I was blessed to take two classes that pertain to the topic. The subject of the first class was Evolutionary Theory/s and its critics, and the subject of the second class was Intelligent Design theory. Through the course of my studies, I gained an intense interest in the human being's understanding of the world around him or her.

Specifically, what does the world around us mean when we interpret it as essentially meaningful or meaningless? How does this affect our engagement with that world? The answers to both questions are found in the details, and there are extraordinarily many details. While the debate over the nature of the world around us touches on a wide variety of fields, astronomy and the information gained from its various sub-fields is particularly enlightening, if for no other reason than that the heavens inspire one of the deepest forms of wonder. A simple fact indeed, but this fact is of the utmost importance for philosophy and for knowledge in general. There is something in the experience of the night, specifically in the night sky, that gives the observer a taste of the sublime. This sublimity sweetly beckons the human person to seek for knowledge.

I learned many things at the conference, but a couple of them stand out. The first is the great contribution that figures in the Church, specifically the Jesuits, have made towards the sciences and especially towards astronomy. Quite simply, it gives a young Catholic a sense of heritage and pride, which is quite helpful in the face of the "ever-ready contemporary critic," who criticizes the Church for things that happened and things that never happened. The second piece of knowledge that was important for me was the understanding of science and theology as building downwards. I found that image particularly helpful. I offer a contrast to the image of building upwards. When building downwards, there is an association with archaeology and digging and discovering things which are already there. The base also gets wider and more questions emerge. The world gets bigger in a sense. The image of building upwards loses the discovery element and in general a building gets smaller as it gets taller. The world of knowledge gets smaller in a sense. Using the former image provides me with an understanding of the world that is refreshing and very far-reaching. It's like looking out at a wide panoramic scene. I can see that there are many questions and answers and that there is so much to discover and probe in the world around us. Ultimately, for me it is a very freeing vision of the world.

If I never read another book or engaged this topic again it would be a blessing just to have my vision of the world enlarged and my eyes more freed. I am entertaining the idea, however, of pursuing philosophy in a serious manner. The content for discernment of that avenue provided by this weekend was rich. The information that I was able to hear and begin to appropriate into my life was great, as I mentioned earlier. In the experience of listening to the discussion, I was also struck by the idea that what was going on before me was a microcosm of the authentic university. There was a group of accomplished professionals from many different disciplines engaging each other and being willing to disagree with one another in the pursuit of a common truth. On top of that, a good spirit was maintained in the agreements and disagreements. It also dawned on me that as an academic one must strike a balance between specialization and community in the pursuit of knowledge. Without specialization, knowledge cannot be deeply penetrated, but without community, specialization leads to blindness. It seems as though for all the universities present in the world, there are not a corresponding number of authentic academic communities. This is a sad state both for academia, and for the student of the 21$^{st}$ century. Blessedly, though, I now know what is possible and how good it is. I am grateful to Dr. Mahfood from Kenrick Seminary for making it abundantly possible to attend these rich experiences and to the ITEST staff for making the conference available. I also thank all of those who offered knowledge from their respective fields for agreement and for disagreement. Peace.

--Vince White, Kenrick-Glennon Seminary. Fall 2007

Thank you for inviting and supporting me so that I could participate in this year's ITEST Symposium. I was very excited to be given this opportunity to learn about the continuing advances in astronomy and cosmology, and to discuss what these advances mean for both the Christian faith and the human being in general. I have always been eager to learn about how and why things are the way they are. This desire for knowledge led me to study physics as an undergraduate. At first I had planned to go into astronomy research, so I spent two summers doing photometry research. Having been raised Catholic as well, God was naturally integrated into my view of the world. It was my discussions with other Christians about the origins of the universe that sparked my interest in my faith, and which first led me to deeper studies of spiritual matters and eventually to test a call to the priesthood. Though I am no longer pursuing a career in the natural sciences, I am still very interested in science, especially where it comes in contact with religion. My progression from scientist to seminarian seems natural for one wishing to understand the world more fully. One begins with the physical and moves to the spiritual, from physics to metaphysics, striving to see how the two combine to form an integrated whole. To see one and not the other is to acknowledge only half of what exists.

The three main speakers were very insightful. Br. Conosolmagno explained how developments in science helped us understand what 'heaven' means. "Going to heaven" is more relational - a supernatural union with God - than an actual physical place. Dr. Barr explained how there are many conditions that seem 'tuned' just right for life, evidence which supports the existence of God. Multiverse theory seems to explain these phenomena independent of any intelligent designer. While there is increasing evidence in particle physics supporting multiverse theories they in no way endanger the need for God. Such theories simply put off the need for God one step further, but cannot avoid Him, since the laws behind a multiverse would be no less specially ordered.

While not officially on the Conference schedule, I found the presentation on the contributions of clergy to science to be fascinating. It demonstrates an unspoken but lived out belief that the Catechism gives: "The humble and persevering investigator of the secrets of nature is being led, as it were, by the hand of God in spite of himself, for it is God, the conserver of all things, who made them what they are" (CCC 159). It also speaks volumes to those who claim that the Church stifles scientific progress, for without the aid of those men of faith and science, progress would have been diminished.

A most important distinction brought up by the responders, was that of what exactly the question of God entailed. Is it about God's existence or about salvation through Christ? The presentations upheld the idea that science is not in conflict with the existence of God and can in fact support it. The question about salvation was not addressed in the presentations themselves, but became a large part of the subsequent discussions. Most problematic with the idea of salvation seemed to be the possibility of other planets with intelligent life. Would they too be in need of salvation though Christ? Would our duty to evangelize extend across the cosmos? Could Christ be enfleshed to them in another way? While these questions extend beyond what science alone can say, they also seem to go past the limits of theology, a science which is limited by what has been divinely revealed. Such speculations are limited by our own prior knowledge. Assuming that to save a separate race of intelligent beings God must again become incarnate as one of them is analogous to the Jews assuming the Messiah must be a temporal ruler that would free them from physical oppression. In truth the Messiah came as God, an idea absolutely foreign to their prior understanding. So too could be they ways of God in his relationship with any other existing rational beings. "Oh, the depth of the riches and wisdom and knowledge of God! How inscrutable are his judgments and how unsearchable his ways! For who has known the mind of the Lord or who has been his counselor?" (Romans 11:33-34) This is not to say that we should not ask these questions. It is to be done with humility and deference to the Church as the interpreter and safeguard of the faith.

One of the most important things that I came away with as it applies to my formation toward priesthood, is the reminder that I need to remain in contact with advances in the sciences. Science greatly influences the way we live and think. Modern philosophies have the tendency to overemphasize the role of science in what we know. The idea that scientific knowledge is the only type of knowledge denies that faith is a legitimate way of knowing. This false dichotomy has caused many to think that to have faith requires one to go against reason. But since both are created by God, there can never be any conflict between these two (CCC 159). They are two wings upon which we can rise to God (Fides et Ratio 1). Again, sometimes the scientist oversteps the limits of science to make assertions that belong to philosophy and theology. It is important to be able to distinguish the regions in which both science and theology can work. Remaining up to date on current scientific advances will help the priest to be able to answer the concerns of his parishioners who hear such claims that seem to falsify the faith.

Thank you again for allowing me to participate in ITEST's discussions.

Kevin Vogel: Kenrick-Glennon Seminary, 2007

# Astronomy/Cosmology Breakthroughs and the God Question

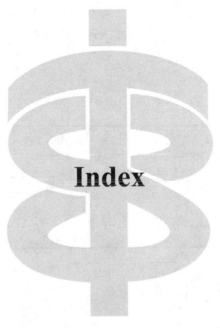

## Index

*Proceedings of the ITEST Symposium - September, 2007*

# A

# B

# C

# D

# E

# F

# G

# H

# I

image of God  62, 148, 149
Imago Dei  148
Incarnation  78, 90, 91, 100, 102, 104, 111, 137, 151
indefectibility  130
infallibility  130
Intelligent Design  21, 25, 44, 59, 63, 84, 109
irreducible complexity  63

# K

kenosis  36, 37, 100
kenotic universe  32, 37

# L

laws of gravity  45
laws of nature  ii, 16, 17, 45, 51, 52, 138
laws of physics  16 - 22, 27, 38, 44, 46 - 54, 117, 139, 146
laws of planetary motion  45
LHC (the Large Hadron Collider)  25, 26
Little Ice Age  119

# M

Metaphysics  33, 61, 68, 70, 71, 83, 123, 128, 131, 134, 150
meteorites  1, 2, 135
modern rationalism  82
modern secularism  34
multiverse  i, 16 - 25, 27, 33, 48 - 54, 69, 70, 72, 87, 88, 101, 116
mystical body  102, 103

# N

natural faith  92
natural philosophy  121, 150
natural science  11
natural selection  39
natural theology  27, 109, 110
neutrons  25, 46, 47
new Adam  102
new creation  104
new Eve  102
new physics  4, 26

# O

Occam's razor  62
Ontologism  83
original sin  9, 100, 102, 104, 137, 149

# P

parallax shift  7
particle physicists  26, 44, 50
particle physics  44 - 46, 50, 52, 111
pathology  32, 39
physical cosmology  3, 32
physical universe  2 - 4, 11, 21, 24, 101, 102, 124
Planck scale  26
planetary observations  3
planetary science  2
planetary systems  2, 9, 10
protons  18, 25, 46, 47

# Q

quantum cosmology  111
quantum mechanics  25, 34, 47, 139
quarks  24

# R

Radiative energy  117
rational proof  59
realist philosophy  86
relationality  87, 88, 90
relativity theory  89, 112, 113
religious experience  131, 132

# S

scientia  11, 12, 87, 121
solar nebulas  10
solar radiation  117
solar system  i, 2, 5, 10, 20
soteriological question  58, 59, 64, 149
soteriology  78, 85, 104
spatial curvature  16, 18, 22, 27
*continues on next page*

166

# Astronomy/Cosmology Breakthroughs and the God Question

# Index of People

*Proceedings of the ITEST Symposium - September, 2007*

# Astronomy/Cosmology Breakthroughs and the God Question

## Participants

*Proceedings of the ITEST Symposium - September, 2007*

## Speakers:

Stephen M. Barr, PhD
Prof. of Physics & Astronomy
Bartol Research Institute
University of Delaware
209 Sharp Lab
Newark, Delaware 19716
smbarr@bartol.udel.edu

Brother Guy Consolmagno, SJ, PhD
Astronomer - The Vatican Observatory
Vatican City  Europe
brother_guy@mac.com

A. Neyle Sollee, MD
Physician/Pathologist
Methodist University Hospital
1620 Galloway Avenue
Memphis, TN 38112
neyle.sollee@gmail.com

## Responders:

Rev. Dr. Steven C. Kuhl
2905 North Shore Drive
East Troy, Wisconsin 53120
Skuhl1@wi.rr.com

Sebastian Mahfood, PhD
Assoc. Prof. - Intercultural Studies
Kenrick Glennon Seminary
5200 Glennon Drive
St Louis, Missouri 63119
mahfood@kenrick.edu

## ITEST Staff:

Thomas P. Sheahen, PhD - Moderator
52 Wanderer Lane
Deer Park, Maryland 21550
Physicist/Vice Dir. ITEST
tsheahen@alum.mit.edu

Marianne Postiglione, RSM
Acting Director: ITEST
Cardinal Rigali Center
20 Archbishop May Drive
St Louis, Missouri 63119
mariannepost@archstl.org

Ms Evelyn P. Tucker
Program Manager - *Exploring the World,
Discovering God (EWDG)*
Cardinal Rigali Center
20 Archbishop May Drive
St Louis, Missouri 63119
evelyntucker@archstl.org

## Attendees:

Professor Benjamin F. Abell
Earth and Atmospheric Sciences
O'Neil Hall Room 300C
St Louis University
221 North Grand Blvd.
St Louis, Missouri 63103

Ms. Kathryn T. Anthony
7704 Marble Canyon Ct.
Fort Worth, Texas 76137
Student - St Gregory's University
Shawnee, Oklahoma

## Attendees:

John F. Cross, PhD
6147 Kingsbury Avenue
St Louis, Missouri 63112
Psychologist - St Louis University
(retired)
crossjf@slu.edu

Mrs. Margaret Craig
23 Manhattan Mews
St Louis, Missouri 63108
Executive Secretary - Anheuser Busch

Robert Z. Greenley, PhD
544 Oak Valley Drive
St Louis, Missouri 63131
Chemist - retired
JBuodby@netscape.com

Sister Marcianne Kappes, CST, PhD
1300 Classen Drive
Oklahoma City, OK 73103-2447
Professor of Religious Studies
St Gregory's University
Shawnee, OK
srmarcianne@stgregorys.edu

Anne McGuire, PhD
824 N. Beard
Shawnee, OK
Professor - St Gregorys' University
acmcguire@stgregorys.edu

Fr. Daniel J. McNamara, SJ
Ateneo De Manila (Manila Observatory)
Quezon City, 1101 Philippines
Jesuit/Astrophysicist
e-mail: daniel@observatory.ph

## Attendees:

Nathan Muenks
Pre-theology student
Kenrick Glennon Seminary
5200 Glennon Drive
St Louis, Missouri 63119

Fr. Earl Muller, SJ, PhD
2701 Chicago Road
Sacred Heart Seminary - Prof. of theology
Detroit, Michigan 48206
Professor of Theology
emuller76@comcast.net

Francisco J. Muller, MS
8025 SW 15th Street
Miami, Florida 33144
Physicist
Varela Academy of Science
fjmuller@bellsouth.net

Mary Ellen Murphy, RSM, PhD
St Joseph College
West Hartford, CT 06117
Professor of Chemistry
mmurphy@sjc.edu

Judge Thad F. Niemira
4924 Sutherland Avenue
St Louis, Missouri 63109
Associate Circuit Judge - retired

Victor Poole III
6831 S. Quaker Avenue
Tulsa, Oklahoma 74136
Student - St Gregory's University
Shawnee, OK 74804

## Attendees:

Greg Pouch, PhD
412 E. Franklin Street
Hudson, Illinois 61748
Geologist
Illinois Wesleyan
gwpouch@gmail.com

Kevin Powell, MD
806 E. Kerr Avenue #202
Urbana, Illinois 61802-2053
kpowell@pol.net

Carla Mae Streeter, OP, ThD, STL
Aquinas Inst. of Theology
23 South Spring Avenue
St Louis, MO 63108
Prof. of Systematic Theology
streeter@slu.edu

Kevin Vogel
1st year theology student
Kenrick Glennon Seminary
5200 Glennon Drive
St Louis, Missouri 63119

Carol Wesley, PhD, ACSW
Director of Practicum
Southern Illinois University - Edwardsville
Edwardsville, Illinois 62026
cwesley@siue.edu

Vince White
Kenrick-Glennon Seminary
5200 Glennon Drive
St Louis, Missouri 63119